INDEPENDENT SACRAMENTAL BISHOPS

Ordination, Authority, Lineage, and Validity

ROB ANGUS JONES

the apocryphile press
BERKELEY, CA
www.apocryphile.org

apocryphile press
BERKELEY, CA

Apocryphile Press
1700 Shattuck Ave #81
Berkeley, CA 94709
www.apocryphile.org

Printed in the United States of America
ISBN 978-1-933993-83-6

DEDICATION

FOR MY PARTNER DAVID, who has supported this project with love and encouragement, even when he did not have the slightest idea what I was going on about.

CONTENTS

ACKNOWLEDGEMENTS

THIS BOOK WOULD SIMPLY NOT BE POSSIBLE without the generosity of time and the sharing of information and insights among my episcopal colleagues:

John Plummer, of the Mission Episcopate of the Theophany, has been a great friend and supporter of my own journey in ministry for years. We have spent many cherished hours by email and in person discussing and reflecting on the challenges and possibilities of the ISM. I am grateful to John for sharing his lines of succession with me. This book owes its publication to John's encouragement, and his editorial suggestions.

Craig Bettendorf, of the Evangelical Anglican Church in America, who first set me on the study of episcopal lineage. I am humbled to have received ordination as a Deacon and a Priest at his hands.

Dr. Joseph Vredenburgh of the Federation of St. Thomas Christians ordained and consecrated me a Bishop. As a fellow cradle Congregationalist, Papa Joe made my ordination an especially unique and precious event.

Darrel Hockley, of the Old Protestant Episcopal Church, one of the most dedicated researchers of Independent Episcopal history

I know. I am in his debt for his many contributions of obscure dates and participant details in particular consecrations.

Philip Garver, of l'Eglise Gnostique, for his tireless efforts and contributions to public knowledge of the French Gnostic Tradition. His generosity in sharing and discussing the fruits of his researches with me has been invaluable.

Bertil Persson, of the Apostolic Episcopal Church, has a legendary repository of Independent Bishop data, and never failed to offer a quick response and warm greetings to even my most obscure questions.

Peter Paul Brennan, of the Ecumenical Catholic Diocese of the Americas, generously provided corrections and additional information on several lines of succession.

Sherrie Albrecht and Deborah Beach Giordano have each prompted me to find ways of explaining the concepts and issues that have become this book, as I have consecrated and welcomed them into the universal College of Bishops.

I have also been truly blessed with conversation over the years with the following bishops, whose perspectives have enriched this book: Rusty Clyma, Tim Cravens, Carlos Florido, John Kersey, Rosamonde Miller, Rusty Smith, Alexis Tancibok, Steven Trivoli-Johnson (of blessed memory), and Wynn Wagner.

And finally an expression of great gratitude to John Mabry for his enthusiasm and encouragement for this project, and seeing it through to publication.

In the final product, this book bears the positive imprints of all these good people. Any mistakes of fact and interpretation are solely my own.

INTRODUCTION

THIS BOOK IS, ABOVE ALL ELSE, A LABOR OF LOVE, and a personal and pastoral exploration of a secluded corner of Christianity. I am an apostolic bishop, shepherding a tiny church, and part of the larger Independent Sacramental Movement (ISM)[1]—sometimes historically called the Independent Catholic churches.

Who are these churches in the Independent Sacramental Movement? We are Churches in that we are self-identified as teaching and celebrating the centrality of Jesus as the Christ, however this is specifically defined in each community. We are sacramental in that we embrace an understanding of Christian life that cherishes the sacraments as channels of grace: baptism, confirmation, marriage, holy orders, Eucharist (communion), anointing the sick and reconciliation (confession)—though we may differ from each other in how many of these sacraments we each practice, and how we understand them. We tend to hold to a 3-fold model of ordained clergy: deacons, priests, and bishops. We are Independent in that we do not belong to one of the more familiar organizations, such as Roman Catholic, Greek Orthodox, or the Anglican Communion—nor do they recognize us as part of them.

Some of us Independent bishops look more like servant leaders; some look more like princes of the church; some look no different from our mainline denominational colleagues; some look a good deal more exotic. We follow a variety of approaches in understanding the exercise of episcopacy, and these approaches together tend to echo the full 2000 years of Church history.

☙

The roots of this book trace to 1998, when the Rt. Rev. Craig Bettendorf asked me to revise and reprint his small apostolic succession brochure. I was a new priest in the Evangelical Anglican Church in America, and working as +Craig's communications director. He gave me his existing Succession brochure, and a small folder of loose papers—some photocopied pages from out-of-print books containing historical lineage information, and some old typed and handwritten notes. He pointed me towards the standard resource books (see Bibliography), and turned me loose on the project.

I was born and raised a Congregationalist, and am by formal education and avocation a historian; this was a whole hidden new world for me. I was utterly unprepared for the humbling visionary passion, the embarrassing venal behaviors, the saintly dedication to ministry, and the unbridled wackiness that I was to encounter among the histories of the bishops of the Independent Sacramental Movement, and their sometimes unsettling fixation on their episcopal lineages. But the more I worked on this research, the more I had a sense of brushing up against a profound and sometimes elusive spiritual reality that these bishops struggled to protect and preserve and rightly pass on, whether they could articulate it or not.

Alongside this elusive spiritual reality, I was fascinated equally by what I can only describe as a pervasive anxiety in the ISM world that casts a shadow over our thoughts and actions, a mocking bogeyman. This bogeyman objects to the possibility that we

ISM clergy and communities might just be "valid" (a technical word meaning "real") and authentic on our own terms, on our own journeys.

In its subtler form, this bogeyman sits on our shoulder as we find ourselves explaining how we're not Roman Catholic but we're still Catholic, or we're not part of the Anglican Communion but we're Anglican, or we're not SCOBA Orthodox but we're Orthodox nonetheless. It's the defensive fallback of "we're *not* them, but we're *like* them." As an Anglican priest trying to build up a parish in the San Francisco area, I faced this one with tiring regularity—how was I different? Why did the tiny progressive jurisdiction I belonged to need to exist—especially in the progressive San Francisco Bay Area? Why did we need a new parish when the Episcopalians had fine parishes nearby—with buildings and paid staff—and the same message of inclusion? Lurking within this was the usually non-spoken question (with its best bogeyman voice): how are you *real* compared to the other guys with buildings and paid clergy and comfy pews and programs? Where's your building?

In its aggressive form, this bogeyman gets in our face with the written and verbal dismissals and condemnations by mainline sacramental leaders and faithful: that we ISM clergy are not "valid" and so our churches are not *authentic*. But at this level, the intent is to frighten the unwitting laity away from us, our ministries, and our efforts to share the Good News.

Sadly, many of us in the ISM have never questioned the right of outsiders to our communities to criticize us as lacking validity; instead we have accepted this criticism and questioning and derision as proper and accurate, and so have made a home for the bogeyman among us. The results are the tragic-comical efforts among us to prove how we're successors of this or that ancient jurisdiction, quivering just a hair's breadth away from being welcomed home. We spend hours and pages defending our authenticity in terms of those jurisdictions—never in our own right and on our own terms. We rob time and energy from actual ministry to joust with the bogeyman in order to prove our worth and authenticity.

This book is an effort to start a new conversation among us about what it means to be "real/valid" Christian communities, "real/valid" sacramental clergy, and "real/authentic" witnesses to the Good News. We ISM leaders must discover how to change the game and exorcise the bogeyman. The alternative is to stay as dogs beneath the dinner table, waiting for crumbs that will never fall.

Nobody should feel that I am writing the last word on the subject. Or for that matter, that I represent the views of every bishop in the movement. My goal is simply to think out loud in these pages about what it means to be Christian bishops who have chosen to exercise our ministries and shepherd our communities in alternative ways outside the mainline jurisdictions.

In my years as ISM clergy what has impressed me most is how powerful this "validity" bogeyman is. As I have reflected on how our colleagues have fretted over this loaded term, I have come to identify three overlapping but distinct themes that tend to get tangled up into the loaded term "valid." I hope in this book to untangle these three issues so we may recognize them clearly and address them properly:

The Sacrament of Ordination—this is the only place the consideration of "validity" legitimately comes into play. The issue here is: was a particular ISM bishop properly ordained? Who owns the ability to determine this for a particular bishop? Why does this matter?

Authority to act as a bishop within a community—this is typically where we ISM folks fight amongst ourselves, as bishops of particular jurisdictions gather to ordain a new bishop for his/her own mission. Who owns the ability to authorize a bishop to provide leadership for a jurisdiction? How do we understand bishops ordained to create communities? Can bishops ever presume leadership in a jurisdiction just because their consecrator(s) lead that jurisdiction?

Episcopal Lineage—the topic that started my journey; a gift of the Holy Spirit to the ISM, this topic creates clouds of confusion over the other two issues, but is a unique and wondrous matter which we'll explore in this book. What—if anything—does it mean for how we proclaim the Good News?

This book will address each of these three issues in turn so that we may better understand what is at stake, and why each matters. Part One will look at the evolution of the concept of bishops, and what it means for a bishop to be properly ordained. We'll turn then to the matter of a bishop's authority, and its sources. Part Two will look at the matter of successions and lineages of bishops, and I will describe Rules of the Road for proper understanding and conveyance of ordinations and consecrations. Part Three will bring into a sharp focus the three themes, and propose a way forward.

Part Four of this book will shift to an examination of the apostolic and inner priesthood lineages in the ISM. In the interest of full disclosure—because I use my own lineage information as the illustrations:

I was consecrated for the episcopacy of the newly formed Free Episcopal Church on 26 July 2001, at a public celebration of the Eucharist at Bishop's Chapel, Watsonville, California. My primary consecrator was Patriarch Maran Mar Joseph Vredenburgh of the Federation of St. Thomas Christians. Mart'a Virginia Vredenburgh and Bishop Joseph Eaton, also of the Federation of St. Thomas Christians, assisted Mar Joseph as co-consecrators. The consecration was according to the Anglican rite. Presenting delegates for the Free Episcopal Church were Rev. Fr. Michael Bonacci, and Mr. David Kerr.

On 16 June 2002, I was privileged to share and merge my lines of apostolic succession in a mutual exchange of consecrations at Saint Brighid's Oratory in Oakland, CA with the Most Rev. John Paul Plummer, of the Mission Episcopate of the Theophany.

On 6 May 2006 I was privileged to share and merge my lines of apostolic succession during a public celebration of the Eucharist at Saint Mychal Judge Old Catholic parish in Dallas, Texas, with John Paul Plummer, of the Mission Episcopate of the Theophany; and James Bryant, of the Holy Orthodox Catholic Church of America, Diocese of Texas.

A note on bishops' names: throughout the following chapters, for those bishops from non-Germanic and non-Romance languages and cultures, I have tried to use the spelling of the bishops' name most closely reflecting their spelling and pronunciation in their native languages. For me, this is a simple matter of respect, and part of engaging these traditions and clergy in their own contexts. I have relied on the presentation of these names in *Lords Temporal, Lords Spiritual* for the majority of these spellings. I have attempted to list in parentheses the common Western name analogs as a point of reference to the standard histories, such as Brandreth, Anson, Pruter/Melton and *Independent Bishops: An International Directory*.

SACRAMENTAL ORDINATION AND EPISCOPAL AUTHORITY

"But if there be any [heresies] which are bold enough to plant [their origin] in the midst of the apostolic age, that they may thereby seem to have been handed down by the Apostles, because they existed in the time of the Apostles, we can say: Let them produce the original records of their churches; let them unfold the roll of their bishops, running down in due succession from the beginning in such a manner that [their first] bishop shall be able to show for his ordainer and predecessor some one of the Apostles or of apostolic men—a man, moreover, who continued steadfast with the Apostles. For this is the manner in which the apostolic churches transmit their registers: as the church of Smyrna, which records that Polycarp was placed therein by John; as also the church of Rome, which makes Clement to have been ordained in like manner by Peter."

—*Tertullian,* DEMURRER AGAINST THE HERETICS, 20 *A.D. 200.*

"Those things, then, concerning spiritual gifts, which are worthy of note, we have set forth. God gave these gifts to people in the beginning in accordance with his will, presenting them with his own image, which had been lost. And now, out of love for all the saints, we have reached the summit of the tradition which is proper for the churches, so that those who are well-taught should guard the tradition which has come down to us now, and which we are now going to consider, and so be confirmed in their knowledge. Because of the error or falling-away that has now come about through ignorance, and through those who are ignorant, the Holy Spirit gives perfect grace to those who rightly believe, so that they should know in what manner those who are pre-eminent in the church should defend and pass on all these things.... Let the bishop be ordained...having been elected by all the people. When he has been named and found pleasing to all, let the people come together with the presbyters, and any bishops who are present, on the Lord's Day. When all give their consent they lay hands on him, and the presbytery stands in silence. And all shall keep silence, praying in their heart for the descent of the Holy Spirit..."

—*Hippolytus, ON THE APOSTOLIC TRADITION, A.D. 235.*

1. WHAT IS A BISHOP?

THE SHORT ANSWER GIVES US A SOLID definition of what is, but little insight into how we got here: Bishops are the Initiators of the Church, the successors to the Apostles and leaders of the Body of Christ, pastors of their own local parishes. Bishops visit local parishes under care of their clergy and preach the Good News as it has always been taught. They baptize new Christians and confirm them; they celebrate the Eucharist (the Lord's Supper); they make new Deacons and Priests from among the baptized, and they receive Religious into vows.

We need a bit longer explanation if we wish to see how this way of organizing and doing Church was an organic process spanning centuries, and how the most central questions concerning the legitimacy of Independent bishops find their beginnings in this same organic process.

WANDERING EVANGELISTS

In the years after the death and resurrection of Jesus, the Apostles and their disciples traveled out across the face of the known world, and preached the Good News as they traveled.

Tradition holds that they traveled as far West as Britain, South into Africa, and East as far as India.

The Apostles were wandering evangelists, bringing a new teaching out into the wider world. Outside Jerusalem there were no church communities, no organizations, no policies and procedures, and no written Gospels or Letters. In a repeated pattern, the Apostles would come to a market square or ruler's public hall, preach the Good News as they received and understood it, perhaps stay in the home of a new believer, and then would travel on to the next destination.

The original authority to preach and teach and live the Gospel came from Christ—whether directly during his lifetime, or afterwards, such as the visionary commissioning experienced by Paul of Tarsus and others. Within a few years of beginning this arduous work, the Apostles themselves seem to have begun training assistants, who would eventually be sent off in new directions to teach on their own, with the authority and teachings derived from their mentors.

Out of this program of wandering and preaching, the first stationary Christian communities were planted. These first communities were quite radical, sharing their worldly goods and food in common, living in the fervor of Jesus' radical message. In each of these new communities, the founding apostle seems to have appointed a leader referred to as an Elder.

We do not know if these first and second generation Elders underwent any formal ordination ceremony in any consistent way—or at all, for that matter. But we do see that at least some were formally approved by the Apostles, or the successors of the Apostles.

A second and apparently parallel office was that of the Deacon (*diakonos*), who acted as the community manager and servant, tending to the worldly needs and arrangements and ministerial outreaches of the community. The Deacon's role of honor was to assist the Elder at celebrations of the Lord's Supper, but more importantly, to be the community's point of on-the-ground ministry to the homeless, sick, orphaned, etc.

In the written records, there are two words for Elder: *episcopos* (where we get the word Episcopal, and the English word Bishop); and *presbyteros* (where we get the word Presbyterian, and the English word Priest). This use of two words has generated centuries of quarreling about what the "real" structure of Church government ought to be (episcopal, or presbyterian), and whether there ought to be a separate Order of Bishops.

☙

Even in the earliest years of Christianity, local communities—and groups within communities—tended to identify themselves as founded by and taught by a particular apostle or successor to a particular apostle. Communities understood themselves as practicing the teaching of Christ *as received by* Andrew (or Philip, etc.). This was common enough that Paul bemoans this tendency in I Corinthians 1:12-13. "Each of you says 'I belong to Paul' or 'I belong to Apollos' or 'I belong to Christ.' Has Christ been divided? Was Paul crucified for you? Or were you baptized in the name of Paul?" (NRSV). It seems there is a human need to understand lineage, belonging, association—how we are personally linked to what matters most to us.

Each of the Apostles proclaimed the words and commands of the Christ as they best recalled them, and each had to teach the Good News in languages and concepts that the locals could understand. This is important to our discussion and to our appreciation of Christianity in general, as we witness the interweaving of human effort with the grace and wisdom of the Holy Spirit. Local traditions naturally emerged out of this context. Dozens of "Gospels" were written, edited, passed on, including the four in our Bibles. We know from their own documents that the early Christians in Gaul were slightly different in belief and practice from the Christians in Antioch or Britain or Jerusalem or India. And even the Gnostic followers of Valentinus could claim their teacher traced his teaching and authority back to St. Paul. From a historical perspective, it is all the more amazing that what we now know as Christianity coalesced and emerged out of this context.

Bishops (Elders), as the successors of the Apostles, continued teaching the Good News of Jesus as they had heard it from the Apostles. Some bishops continued to be vagabonds, sent further out into the world to proclaim the Good News, and establish new communities of believers as they traveled. The bishops were commissioned to this missionary wandering—they were not ordained for existing communities. They were understood as the authorized keepers of the apostolic tradition.

ࣙ

As the local Christian communities grew, bishops were increasingly able (and encouraged) to settle down as permanent Elders, and as their work prospered, would often become pastors to more than one community, especially in the urban areas within the Roman Empire. Ironically just as many bishops were able to leave the unstructured life of wandering evangelist behind, some were now forced to travel throughout a region to minister to the faithful in multiple small communities.

Out of this a new practice emerged, borrowed from the model of Roman civil governance, and dictated by necessity: the bishops began to designate liturgical and pastoral stand-ins (literally, vicars), who could—but only under the bishop's authority—baptize, and celebrate the Lord's Supper, and preach and teach in the bishop's place. These Vicars of the Bishop became known as Presbyters, with *episcopos* referring only to the Bishop. So the Church grew from having one Bishop (Elder) for each community, to having one Priest (Elder) per community with one Bishop over multiple communities—with each priest able to act only within the authority given to him by his Bishop. By this point, sadly, the priests and bishops seem (almost) all to have been males.

There is an interesting vestige that testifies to the reality that Bishops and Priests were originally one and the same Order of ministry: several apostolic successions have been restored by having a synod of Priests lay hands on an elected Priest and thereby making that person a Bishop. We'll look more deeply at this in chapter 3.

ꙮ

We must recognize that alongside this evolving episcopal model of doing church, the records show that our earliest faith ancestors practiced several other organizational models. One of these was more akin to Paul's experience on the Damascus Road: an angel, or Christ, or the Holy Spirit, or Holy Wisdom (Sophia), would create a community or raise up a pastor by direct revelation and commissioning, without any outer stamp of approval by one of the Apostles or their successors. (This is important to our story later on.) Another model is more familial/tribal, as we see in the Jerusalem Church, which was led by Jesus' brother James and other relatives after his death. And there seem to be more egalitarian models where leadership was shared more democratically or synodally. So the Bishop model of doing Church was not the only one, and perhaps not even at first the majority model. But it was the one with the best chances to succeed in the Roman world.

BISHOPS GET ORGANIZED

Through the first two hundred years, the sense of territory and scope of authority for a bishop varied across the Christian world, and was a living and evolving concept, growing organically alongside the concept of the role and office of the bishop. The sense of who and what the bishop was, and what the bishop was responsible for, developed in complexity as the numbers of Christians grew. The churches looked to the most effective organizational model in their lives: the Roman civil government. And they—consciously or unconsciously—adopted a number of the 'best practices' of the Roman world.

As the years passed, and one bishop succeeded another as leader of a community or group of communities, the concept of a "succession" began to be formulated. As the eyewitnesses to Jesus' life on earth died out, and the first generation of disciples of the eyewitnesses also died out, it was critical to the followers of the Way to know they were getting true and complete teachings about Jesus, and true and complete continuation of Jesus' own instruction.

Out of this necessity, the key concept of Apostolic Succession first developed. Initially it meant the handing down of the unaltered *teaching* received from the Apostles, and writers spoke in a more focused way about the Apostolic Tradition (though, as we've noted, there were several 'Traditions' that tightly overlapped, but retained local variations). Apostolic Succession as Apostolic Tradition ensured that a community stood in a line of rightly taught and rightly teaching Elders/Bishops.

It is incidentally this earliest layer that the Protestant Reformers hearkened back to in their claims to rediscover a "scriptural episcopacy" for their leadership after they broke with Rome and worked to return to what they believed were the original apostolic teachings and doctrines.

In this view of Succession as Tradition, a Bishop is only a Bishop by standing in a line of teachers that is believed to reach back to the Apostles themselves *and* teaching what was believed to be always taught by the Apostles. Succession in a line of teachers and authority to be in that line as an Elder were one and the same. There is but one universal College of Bishops, all of equal rank and stature and authority, because all are the co-equal vessels of the true teaching. And any interpretation of understanding must come from the college of bishops *in their entirety*. The bishops altogether speak as the voice of the Church. This is the origin of the concept of the 'ecumenical council,' and the unseemly disagreements down the centuries about what has been truly ecumenical (meaning, all the world).

In those areas that were most heavily influenced by the Roman love of practical clarity and lack of ambiguity (the Latin West), a small logical step changed the understanding of succession. If bishops were consecrated because they rightly taught what was held to be (in the years before the approval of a single collection of scriptures) the unaltered Gospel, then bishops could be considered true bishops if they followed in direct succession to rightly teaching bishops—because in their ordination vows they promised to retain the unaltered teachings as they received them.

In the West, the Apostolic Succession was morphing into a chain of rightly-made bishops, and the emphasis shifted from the lineage of teaching, to the lineage of bishops. This is a crucial detail, and the small change in nuance opened the door to all manner of concerns and issues for the Churches in the West ever after as we will see in later chapters.

cs

Whether the apostolic seal of approval rested with the received tradition or the chain of succession, for the majority of the Christian world the bishops as local and regional Elders had emerged as the leaders of the faithful, the teachers of the Good News, and the Initiators (through baptism, confirmation, and ordination) of the faithful. All authority in the Church was understood to flow "downwards" from the bishops, who, as successors of the Apostles, were Vicars of the Christ in the world, and mediators of the gifts and graces of the Holy Spirit into the community. And so priests and deacons could only perform their spiritual duties if they were authorized by the bishop to do so. This perfectly mirrored the Roman civil model of delegated authority.

Likewise, bishops had organized themselves as synods within regions, and a bishop was only authorized to do the work of a bishop by the synod of bishops in his region. A bishop was now made for the sole purpose of pastoral oversight of a diocese or territory. The synod, acting as a visible portion of the universal college of bishops, gave authority to a new bishop to act as one of the college. This shift also signaled the end of the bishop as wandering evangelist in the wider world, since such people were unregulated, and unknown by the local regions through which they passed.

CONSTANTINE UNIFIES THE CHURCH

Thus far, we have completely ignored a critical factor in shaping Christianity: the centuries of persecutions, executions, and the legal status of Christians as heretics. Whole generations of Christian leaders, thinkers, and mystics were often wiped out by an Emperor's need for a scapegoat, or a changing mood about religious tolerance. Christians topped the list as fodder for lions in the forum. Much of Church life was conducted under the radar, and much of what developed was of necessity to safeguard the community in the event of renewed persecution.

All of this changed when Constantine determined to make Christianity the unifying religious force of the Roman Empire, and Christianity was declared by law to be a State Religion.

☙

To bring the complex variety of Christian expression into a useful focus, Constantine convened the world's first Ecumenical Council, in Nicaea. In his pragmatic Roman mind, Christianity had all the right stuff to be a State Religion, but there were too many variations, too many versions. He had to have a single homogenous version of the faith that could be everywhere the same, with a single set of sacred texts, a single test of faith, a single cadre of approved supervisors to deliver this teaching, and administer the same sacraments. The Council was directed by Constantine himself to hammer out a comprehensive statement of the Good News, and to identify the parameters of the Tradition.

Uncharitable scholars have viewed this as the creation of a sort of lowest-common-denominator version of the original Christian message. More likely, the better organized and more politically savvy groups practicing what would later be called Orthodoxy emerged as the one approved variety of Christianity.

After Christianity became the State religion of Rome, the notion and shape of authority was solidified. Bishops were deputized as the key disseminators of this centralized Tradition. And the full force of Roman civil law was now employed to systematically eradicate all other variations of Christian practice and belief.

Bishops, like the pagan priests and pontiffs before them, in fact became agents of the State. Out in the Roman provinces and rural areas bishops were often deputized as Roman civil governors (exarchs and eparchs) as well, alongside their spiritual duties. It is not accidental that bishops began to take on some of the trappings of Roman civil leaders: the wearing of imperial/senatorial purple, the use of the bishop's ring (which began life as a signet ring to seal civil documents); and a developing sense of rulership over the faithful, the first seeds of self-understanding as "Princes of the Church."

ꟻ

Once bishops became agents of the State as well as the keepers of the Gospel, Roman and Church law needed to be precise, so there was no doubt who was a *real* bishop. The Eastern and Western parts of the Church each evolved and developed their own rules for making a bishop, and for defining who was a legitimate bishop. We'll return to this in chapter 3.

Down the centuries, as the Roman civil model of top-down authority hardened into the spiritual hierarchy of the Churches, this notion of authority became quite rigid. No longer could bishops wander abroad in the world, preaching and teaching where the Spirit led. Instead, they were confined to territorial boundaries, which were typically identical to Roman civil boundaries. If clergy traveled, they had to get permission from the local bishops to function as clergy within the territory they visited. If bishops were deprived of their own territory by war, barbarian invasions, or politics, or determination of heresy, and if they were then forced to wander, they did so now as outsiders, and pariahs.

Equally important, the etiquette for determining who was a real bishop coalesced during this period. Regional synods of bishops naturally assumed the proper authority for determining the validity of all clergy within their regional boundaries. This etiquette also determined that other synods of bishops refrained from questioning the validity of each others' clergy. The common assumption was that each synod followed Tradition and common practice to ensure the Sacrament of Ordination was rightly conducted.

ONE CHURCH, MANY CHURCHES

Through the centuries, through politics and ecclesial events, the single homogeneous version of the faith diverged again into the vast Western, Byzantine and Oriental strands, each with many smaller threads of local and regional custom, nuanced teaching, unique versions of the scriptures and interpretations of Tradition. For several centuries, one of the largest threads (in numbers and geography) of the Christian Tradition was, in fact, the Assyrian Church of the East (the so-called Nestorian Church), which stretched from the western shores of the Mediterranean Sea to the Pacific Ocean, from Turkey through China to the Pacific Ocean.

Through the natural organization of regional bishops into synods, and the Roman imperial model of centralization of authority, the Church came to recognize that there were five episcopal locations that had a primacy of place ("first among equals") amongst their colleagues, due to the importance of their communities and their spiritual importance overall to Christendom. These five episcopates were elevated to the role of patriarchates over all the Christians resident in their geographic areas.

The five original ancient Patriarchates are: Jerusalem (which long since lost its original episcopal succession), Antioch, Alexandria, Constantinople, and Rome. By Tradition, all bishops derive their ordination from one of these five Patriarchates, as direct successors to the Apostles. (Later ethnic patriarchates in turn derive from these five.)

A more helpful way of identifying the major fault lines between the Traditions of apostolic Christendom is used by Roman and Byzantine writers, and while biased, does reveal the major historic liturgical, political, and administrative boundaries:

Western Apostolic Churches—this group includes those Churches that can trace their primary succession from the Patriarch (Pope) of Rome: principally the Roman Catholic, Anglican, and Old Catholic jurisdictions.

Chalcedonian/Byzantine Orthodox—this group includes those Eastern Churches which adhere to the 7 Ecumenical Councils, and politically have allied themselves historically with the Eastern emperors and doctrinally with the decisions of the Patriarch of Constantinople: the Ecumenical Patriarchate, Greek, Greek Orthodox Patriarchates of Alexandria and Jerusalem, Cyprus, Russian (and the newly re-emerging ethnic churches subsumed by the Russian Patriarchate during the Soviet era), Romanian, Serbian, Bulgarian, Georgian, Czech, Albanian, Polish, and Finnish jurisdictions.

Oriental Orthodox (or "Monophysite")—this grouping contains those Eastern Churches that recognize only the first three or four Ecumenical Councils. These include those deriving from the Patriarch of Antioch: the St. Thomas Christians, Syriac, Armenian, and Malankara Syrian; and those deriving from the Patriarch (Pope) of Alexandria: Coptic & Ethiopian.

Church of the East (or "Nestorian")—this group consists of the Assyrian Church of the East.

"Uniate" Churches—a commonly (and incorrectly) used term to refer to those Eastern churches that have, while retaining their original Orthodox liturgical and spiritual life, aligned themselves administratively under the Roman patriarch: (Greek) Melkite, Armenian Catholic, Chaldean Catholic. These are commonly parallel jurisdictions to those remaining under the administrative leadership of an Orthodox jurisdiction.

2. CHRISTIAN INITIATION

BEFORE IT BECAME THE STATE RELIGION of Rome, Christianity primarily was a Mystery religion (the central messages, meanings, and revelations were secrets known only to the full members) and it existed side-by-side with a number of other Hellenistic Mystery religions. In the Hellenistic mind, a person could naturally belong to and participate in the Mysteries of more than one religion. Christianity learned from and absorbed something of the features of its spiritual milieu—though it rejected the practice of participating in multiple Mystery paths, considering its own Mysteries to supersede all others.

Like the other Mystery faiths, Christianity required a lengthy period of training before aspirants could be initiated into the community. For Christians, the period of preparation was normally several years, and this initiation was through full immersion baptism, literally a foretaste of dying and rising into new life. This was a training of adults, as children and infants were not able to receive and understand the Mysteries.

Christianity, in fact, understood itself as an initiatic path. Even today, our church liturgies among the Orthodox, Catholic, and Anglican bodies reflect the mark of the initiatic origins. The first half of the liturgy is commonly also known as the Mass of the Catechumens (one who is receiving elementary instruction). During this first half of the liturgy, those who were undergoing instruction in the Christian faith, but were not yet baptized (initiated), were allowed to hear the Good News preached, to pray, and to sing hymns. At the end of this first half of the liturgy (usually just before the confession of faith), everyone not baptized was ushered out of the sanctuary.

Only then was the central Mystery revealed. Also in the West called the Mass of the Faithful, this second half of the liturgy is where the great Mysteries of Christ's life, death, and resurrection were revealed again, on the altar. This is where the initiates into the Body of Christ were able to give thanks (the root meaning of "eucharist"), and to participate in the revelation of God's love.

For Christians there are three initiatic mysteries/sacraments that were and are rites of passage, literally a crossing over a threshold, on our journey into Christ. As such, these three initiations can only be received once.[2] Baptism and Chrismation or Confirmation mark us as members of the Body of Christ, participating not only in the Resurrection of Christ but also in the descent of the Holy Spirit at Pentecost. Ordination likewise marks those ordained as keepers and leaders of the Mysteries.

Mysteries had to be rightly performed and rightly received. So the Church had to define: who was actually baptized and eligible to witness the Mysteries; and who was rightly ordained and authorized to lead, or celebrate the Mysteries. It is revealing that in the Eastern Church, we speak about the Mysteries when referring to baptism, ordination, etc.; while in the Western Church, we speak about sacraments. The Eastern Church retains this additional hint of our collective initiatic roots.

BAPTISM

Baptism was and is the cornerstone, the initiation into the Church. Baptism itself originally was conducted in a way that would look very odd indeed to most modern eyes: for those communities not located close to living (running) water, the baptism was conducted in a small tank the shape and size of a sarcophagus. The person being baptized—whether in living water or in the coffin-shaped tank—was naked and was immersed, submerged, and held under while the words of baptism were solemnly spoken over her or him. The experience was truly intended to convey the understanding of dying to the old life, and being reborn into the new life of the Body of Christ.

Then, as now, the person was baptized into Christ, and not to any particular local body, sect, denomination, or jurisdiction. We are not baptized as Catholics or Anglicans or Melkites; we are baptized as Christians.

Since the beginning, Christian teaching has always recognized that any baptized Christian, as a keeper of the Good News, can perform the rite of baptism. Any initiate into the Body of Christ can initiate another into the Body. This is a perfect example of Martin Luther's teaching on the priesthood of all believers. It's not just a pretty phrase—it points to the level of responsibility and authority given to us by this sacrament, and to our relationship to the Holy Spirit, who acts through the one performing the baptism.

As with all the Mystery religions, initiation into Christianity was considered to create a permanent change in a person—we sometimes talk in that wonderful medieval language about "an indelible mark" on a person's soul. One may renounce one's faith, but the experience of initiation through baptism remains in one's person the rest of his or her life.

CHRISMATION/CONFIRMATION

Confirmation, in the incisive words of the *Encyclopedia of Catholicism*, is "a sacrament seeking a theology" (p. 349).

In the beginning of Christianity, when all baptism was adult baptism, the final step in the rite of passage was the anointing of the newly-baptized person with chrism, an aromatic oil set aside for this purpose. The chrismation (anointing with chrism) of the new Christian was done by the bishop as a sealing of the gift of baptism.

Over time, two things happened that forever altered the process: bishops became regional instead of local community Elders; and communities began baptizing their children.

When bishops became regional Elders, they visited each local community less frequently, and one of their roles as successor of the Apostles was then to confirm the rite of baptism performed by their local priests. This was part quality check, to ensure that the new Christian had been rightly taught the Gospel; and part ritual check, to ensure that the new Christian had been rightly baptized. The sign of this confirming of the new Christian was the anointing of the person with chrism. So the single act of baptism in water and anointing with oil was split into two parts: the first allowed to be performed by the priest as vicar of the bishop; the second reserved for the bishop.

Over time, Eastern and Western practice diverged. In the Orthodox world, chrismation has tended to return to its place as a final act at baptism. Orthodoxy views baptism as a participation in the death and resurrection of Jesus; and chrismation as a participation in the coming of the Holy Spirit.

Western practice has tended to push confirmation further away from baptism, and has related it (since most all baptism is still infant baptism) to the person's coming to the 'age of reason'—which oddly for Roman Catholics is often set as young as age seven! In this way, the rite of confirmation is seen as a person embracing the baptismal vows made on her/his behalf, and becoming fully and voluntarily a member of the Christian community. While the proper minister of this sacrament is the bishop, in both East and West it is commonly and appropriately celebrated by the parish priest as the bishop's Vicar. In the West, as in the East, many traditions do still anoint the person with chrism at their confirmation.

The importance here for our discussion is that the bishop, both East and West, plays the critical role as Initiator of the new Christian, whether as infant or as youth or adult. The message of this rite is the empowerment of the new Christian as full member of the Body of Christ.

ORDINATION/CONSECRATION

Ordination, too, is a rite of initiation, into the leadership of the Church. It is a rite of passage for those set apart to proclaim the Good News, to reveal the Mystery of Eucharist, and to be empowered to baptize (initiate) new believers (though any baptized believer can baptize). It's here that over time the Church will need to understand a distinction between those *empowered* through the Mystery/Sacrament of Ordination to lead the Church, and those *authorized* by the Church upon their ordination to lead the Church. We'll return to this in the next chapter.

There is no recorded demonstration by Jesus or his Apostles of how to ordain leaders, and we are left to guess at whether Jesus had any formal initiation event for the Apostles as he commissioned them. The Church looked to the events of Pentecost to understand that it is the Holy Spirit who brings the empowerment of ordination to the one being ordained; it is the bishops who provide the conduit and witness for this empowerment to enter into the candidate.

Ordination to the Major Orders (Deacon, Priest, and Bishop) is an extension of our Baptism and Confirmation, a call to be set aside as particular servants of the Good News. To serve the community of priests that is the Church.

There are other distinctions of clergy and laity, but they are not expressions of the *Sacrament of Orders*. Laity may function non-sacramentally as clerics, acolytes, exorcists, doorkeepers, and lectors; psalmists, and cantors. These collectively are historically known as Minor Orders. (A Subdeacon has at various times been considered as either a Minor Order or a Major Order.) The Minor Orders originated as assigned tasks within the local community—which over time became functions that initiated community members were consecrated to perform.

For both Minor and Major Orders (and the taking of vows as Religious), the person entering the ministry is said to be consecrated to this service. To consecrate is to set aside for holy purposes. For Major Orders, the person is also said to be ordained—the specific rite by which the person is consecrated, and the Holy Spirit is invoked over the person.

Within the Major Orders, the Archdeacon, Archpriest, Archimandrite, Archbishop, Metropolitan, Patriarch, and Pope are administrative distinctions, denoting special functions assigned to a Deacon, Priest, or Bishop. Thus, the Roman Catholic and Coptic Popes are sacramentally bishops absolutely equal to every other apostolic bishop around the world.

Sacramental consecration as a bishop has several integrated meanings. It is the descent of the Holy Spirit upon the new bishop, to be received into the universal fellowship of bishops as elders of the church and witnesses to the Good News; it is to become Vicars of Christ. The several co-consecrating bishops are symbols of the participation of the whole college of bishops and the inherent collegiality of the episcopate. And finally, consecration and ordination as a bishop is an initiation into a thread of Christian tradition as a keeper of that tradition, and an assimilation to Christ, who is the one and only Priest.

For the purposes of our discussion of Ordination, we'll very briefly look at the each of the Major Orders in turn, as they were originally practiced:

Deacons—are ordained to supervise the right use of the worldly goods of the local community, and actively work in ministries of service and presence between the local communities and those who are in need in the world at large. Deacons give voice to the voiceless, and make visible the real needs of those whom society makes invisible: widows, orphans, the poor, etc. By extension today, this ministry is coming to be understood in broader terms, and Deacons are called on to speak for the earth, as stewards of the resources of our planet, and as kin of all our non-human sisters and brothers. Deacons at worship proclaim the Gospel and serve at the Communion Table.

Priests—are ordained to celebrate the sacraments (Baptism, Eucharist, etc.), provide pastoral care and oversight for the local communities (or ministries or chaplaincies), to teach the Gospel, and lead by example. Priests today are called on to reveal the whole earth as Sacred, and all of life as Holy. They still are the symbolic deputies of the bishop, and so remind the local communities of their membership in the whole Church.

Bishops—are ordained as pastoral leaders. Bishops fulfill their ancient role as initiators of the faithful: baptizing, confirming, commissioning, and ordaining. As such, Bishops ensure that those who are initiated are ready and worthy. Bishops ensure that the Gospel is rightly and fully revealed, that ministers and communities and ministries are spiritually nurtured.

Ancient evidence indicates that originally a Deacon could be ordained a Bishop without first having to be ordained a Priest. This is doubtless a remnant of the earliest years of the Church when there were only Deacons and Elders (*episkopoi* = Bishops).

3. WHO IS A REAL BISHOP?

AS WE SAW IN CHAPTER 1, AS THE CHURCH GREW, and especially later as it emerged as the Roman State Religion, it became absolutely critical to know if any particular bishop was truly a bishop, properly ordained, and authorized to lead the Church. The bishop was and is the foundation of all the Church's mysteries/sacraments, and is considered to be the actual means of transmitting God's grace into the Church. It is the bishop who makes the priests and deacons who preside at the baptisms, Eucharist, etc. By definition, if the bishop is not rightly made, none of the clergy can be rightly made by him, and none of the Mysteries celebrated by the clergy are rightly done.

The Synods of bishops responsible for ensuring the validity of their own bishops in these early centuries were faced with the complexity of sharing the world with leaders from other competing Christian schools of belief, and bishops of unknown spiritual pedigree wandering through their territories. The simplicity of the original person-to-person vouchsafing of validity was repeatedly shaken, and bishops began to work to define more carefully and universally the concept and process of validity.

Note: Since Orthodox/Catholic bishops were all males after Constantine, I will use the masculine pronoun for simplicity and accuracy.

One example will illustrate the predicament of defining "real" bishops from heretics or imposters: In the early 2nd entury there was an exceptionally gifted theologian and teacher named Valentinus. He belonged to and led a school of Christianity with views that diverged from the Orthodox school. Valentinus could factually claim to be a disciple of Theudas, who was in turn a disciple of the Apostle Paul. Thus his claim for Apostolic Tradition and teaching authority was equal to the prominent Orthodox Christian bishops of his day. Valentinus narrowly missed being elected the Bishop of Rome (the Pope).

The Orthodox communities recognized that because of the number of heterodox priests and teachers like Valentinus, the old definition of a bishop as a disciple of an Apostle would no longer do; they needed a more comprehensive and subtle measure of what made a real (a.k.a. Orthodox) bishop.

The making of a bishop the right way—giving that indelible mark on the soul—would come to have several very specific features. And defining this process served two vital needs: to know that bishops of the Orthodox Church were rightly made; and to exclude the possibility, at least in Orthodox minds, that those outside the Orthodox school could have rightful bishops of their own.

This has set the precedent for discussion down to the present: politically and numerically dominant denominations continue to use their relative position to define the terms of the discussion, whether it pertains to the validity of other denominations' sacraments, or the "right" social, moral, theological, or political positions.

CYPRIAN & THE EASTERN DEFINITION

St. Cyprian of Carthage (died 258) was crucial to the consolidation of Orthodoxy, by teaching that the bishops as a synod were the foundation of the Church. Reacting to the schisms and heresies of his day, and in the midst of Roman persecutions, he championed the vision of one unified Church as the Body of the faithful in Christ. It was Cyprian who first articulated the doctrine of the absence of grace everywhere but within the one True Church. While he did not stress any particular details of apostolic succession, he did emphasize that the bishops were the successors of the Apostles, and the sole legitimate interpreters of the Apostolic Tradition.

From this, he reasoned that if a bishop disagreed with the Tradition or his fellow bishops, he was no longer part of the one Church, and thus, had removed himself from grace. A bishop was only a bishop while in accord and communion with his fellow bishops, and while teaching the apostolic faith.

Cyprian further taught and insisted that no episcopal seat gave a bishop any governing authority over any other bishop. So the bishop of Rome, or Antioch, or Alexandria had no special governing authority over his fellow bishops. It was only the full roster of bishops meeting in synod who could speak and act with authority over themselves as a whole.

For Cyprian, the *ability* to be a bishop (given by receiving the Mystery of Ordination) was inextricably bound to one's *authority* to be a bishop (granted by the synod of bishops, as a specific jurisdiction). Both were determined by one's standing in the one Church. A bishop who was not a part of the one Church had no authority to be a bishop, and had no ability to be a bishop (at least in theory). This notion logically followed from Cyprian's teaching that outside the one Church, as defined by those within it, there is no grace, and no salvation. And thus, one could not *be* a bishop, since the bishop is, as the Vicar of Christ, the channel of grace.

Out of this, we can see that the number of bishops in the East who were actually wandering about unaffiliated was usually restricted to those former Orthodox who had been cast out for heresy, and the unknown number of non-Orthodox bishops. They were by this Cyprianic definition no longer bishops.

AUGUSTINE & THE WESTERN DEFINITION

About 150 years later St. Augustine of Hippo (384—430) faced new and different social and economic realities, and believed that he articulated and developed Cyprian's ecclesiology in greater detail. For Augustine and the Western Church, it was no longer enough to talk about being in accord and communion with one's fellow bishops.

It was Augustine who focused the teaching on the indelible character of ordination. He identified four criteria to be used to determine whether an ordination is rightly done, or to use the technical word, *valid*:

1. Form: The ordination of a Bishop must take place in a public setting (by custom it is usually in Eucharistic worship, though the form of ordination is in truth just the prayer of consecration), using an appropriate Order of ordaining a Bishop. In this we see the powerful symbol that the bishop is made in and for the Church. An ordination in secret or apart from the church's worshipping community is usually considered invalid.

2. Matter: Ordination must be by actual physical laying on of hands. Praying over the candidate is not sufficient.

3. Minister: The ordaining bishop(s)—the one(s) laying on hands—previously must have been validly ordained within the Apostolic Succession.

4. Intention: The intent of the physical laying on of hands during the ordination liturgy must be to ordain and consecrate the person to the episcopate of the One Holy Catholic and Apostolic Church. Intent must be present both on the part of the ordaining bishop(s) and the ordinand: to teach what the Church has always taught. This criterion is meant to negate claims made that a person was ordained for the episcopate during the laying on of hands for healing, for example. Likewise, those who demonstrably do not intend to teach what the Church has always taught are not technically valid bishops by this definition.

The Augustinian view, taken to its logical conclusion, makes it possible to view episcopacy as a personal possession, rather than as a state of being in the church. This is uncharitably sometimes referred to as the "pipeline theory" of Orders, since it makes becoming a bishop rather like turning on a faucet. In the Augustinian view, once a bishop, always a bishop—regardless of one's standing in the one Church.

The Eastern Churches rejected Augustine's teachings on this and other subjects, preferring Cyprian's position to this day.

Augustine made it possible and necessary to now speak about the *authority* to be a bishop (assignment to a jurisdiction) as distinct from the *ability* to be a bishop (receipt of the Sacrament of Ordination). If a person was made a bishop, and received the indelible mark of holy Orders, then what happened if that person left the one Church? What if that bishop lapsed into schism or heresy? Or in later centuries, what if a bishop protested Church policy or politics, and left and founded an independent jurisdiction?

We in the West (Roman Catholics, Anglicans, and Old Catholics) have continued to rely most heavily on the Augustinian model, for better and worse.

A REAL SACRAMENT: VALIDITY

Both Cyprian and Augustine focused on what makes an ordination *valid*. Validity pertains to whether or not the ritual actions and intentions actually create a sacrament, and are not simply theater. If it is a valid sacrament, then it becomes an actual means of grace. If it is not a valid sacrament, then however edifying it might be, it is not technically able to be a channel of grace.

It is important to point out that for both Cyprian and Augustine, a bishop is only made in the church, and only for the church, and it is the Holy Spirit that makes the bishop during the sacrament. The sacrament of making a bishop must be accompanied by the church's authorization to lead a jurisdiction, granted by the responsible synod of bishops. Bishops are made in order to lead and serve a specific community or group of communities, and participate in the synod of bishops.

It is essential to remember that both Cyprian and Augustine were speaking *within* their communions, and *for* their communions. While they were writing and teaching, numerous other Christian communions existed alongside, but outside of the Orthodox/Catholic communion. We must remember that within the concept of validity is the understanding that it is an *internal* definition, owned and adjudicated by those within a communion and used to vouchsafe Orders for the communion. There is no other legitimate voice in the conversation.

This is an enormous shift from the earliest days of bishops as vagabonds for Christ, who planted and built up new communities as they traveled. But this shift was required in order to draw a clear line between those within and those outside the boundaries of the Church and its grace.

In our day, the concept of validity is much discussed as various sacramental communions struggle over the ordination of women. For example, for Roman Catholics and the Orthodox, a woman is not able to be ordained because of her gender, since the form of the Sacrament of Ordination in the traditional Roman and Orthodox definitions requires a baptized male.

☙

Validity seems simple enough when it is played out within clear boundaries, among and for one's own constituents: the Episcopal Church in the US properly determines the validity of its own bishops (but witness the tempest created as sister jurisdictions within the Anglican Communion attempt to improperly enforce their own criteria on the ECUSA); Roman Catholic bishops in their various provinces determine validity within those provinces, in consultation with their Patriarch; Russian Orthodox bishops in their various geographical exarchates determine validity within those regions, in consultation with their Patriarch, and so on.

The situation gets more interesting when a group parts ways with its former affiliation and becomes self-determining. In the West, when the Dutch Catholics withdrew their communities from the Roman Catholic jurisdiction, they then became solely responsible for ensuring the validity of those ordained with their new Old Catholic communion. It was no longer the responsibility or ability of Rome to monitor or make any determination of Old Catholic orders. Likewise, when the Catholic Church in England withdrew from Rome and became the Church of England, they also took on the responsibility for ensuring their own validity, and Rome no longer had authority for this oversight. We'll revisit these two events in the next chapter.

Note that in both cases, the new Anglican and Old Catholic jurisdictions (as well as the vast majority of their sacramental colleagues in other jurisdictions) understood that their sacraments and orders were *able to be valid* not because they were formerly Roman Catholic; but rather because they shared in the ancient succession of ordinations from the Apostles conveyed down through time. What made Old Catholic and Anglican sacraments *valid* were those jurisdictions' own exercised responsibility to ensure that the apostolic transmission was rightly maintained.

☙

I intentionally reference the Old Catholics and the Anglicans because the way these separations played out on the religious stage in the West provided the cultural context for the emergence of the first Independent jurisdictions in Great Britain, France, and the United States. We'll return to the concept of validity as a key ISM concept in Chapter 6.

DOING IT RIGHT: REGULARITY AND LICEITY

Implicit in Cyprian and Augustine, and spelled out over the next centuries, is the parallel question of Church discipline. From this perspective, the Church judges whether a sacrament is *regular*, or *licit*. Roman and Anglican usage differ on what these terms mean.

For Roman Catholics, a sacrament is *licit* if it follows the general rules of the church for the conduct of the sacrament (type of bread, etc). A sacrament is *regular* if the recipient is able to partake of the sacrament according to the rules of the Church (age, capacity, etc.).

Anglicans use the term *regular* to encompass both the Roman sense of licit and regular.

A sacrament may be valid, but be irregular and/or illicit. ISM clergy are sometimes considered valid but illicit/irregular by Romans and Anglicans, although both communions generally remain silent on the issue. Typically this means that the ISM liturgy took place without the consent of a Roman or Anglican bishop, and outside the authority—yet within the geographical jurisdiction—of a Roman or Anglican bishop.

A sacrament may be regular and/or licit, but be invalid because of some defect. For instance the Liberal Catholic Church (in many of its branches) has been said by some non-LCC Christians to depart from teaching what the church has always taught. Therefore, according to these outsiders, when LCC bishops make new LCC bishops, even if the ordination is both licit and regular, it could be argued to be invalid because the intentions of the consecrators and ordinand are not to uphold the traditional teachings, but rather to teach unique LCC doctrines. Likewise, the consecrations of bishops for the original Order of Corporate Reunion have been considered by outsiders to be regular and licit, but invalid because the ordinations took place in secret, rather than at a public liturgy.

It is essential to recognize that definitions of regularity and liceity were created *within* communions, and *for* communions to monitor their own sacraments. Determining whether a sacrament is regular and licit parallels determining whether a sacrament is valid: responsibility is owned by the communion in which the sacrament occurs. There is no other legitimate voice in the conversation.

MAKING IT RIGHT: CONDITIONAL SACRAMENT

Once this nature of the sacrament has been defined, questions arise. What if:

The sacrament was later discovered to not be done properly (and so is not actually the sacrament, and imparts no indelible mark)?

The Minister of the sacrament has a shadow of doubt cast upon his (or her) validity as a minister of the sacrament? Meaning, we can't be certain that the sacrament imparted its mark?

The recipient of the sacrament has a shadow of doubt cast upon her or his intention to receive the sacrament (or in the case of infant baptism, the parents or guardians of the infant)? Meaning, we can't be certain that the sacrament was actually received?

These questions vexed the Churches. Through the centuries, there have been political opportunists who sought Orders for political and economic advantage. There have been con men who wandered into a new region and pretended to be bishops. There have been legitimate requests by clergy to leave one communion and move to another in earnest faith—such as conversions from Catholicism to Orthodoxy. There have been oversights and mistakes. In a time in the world when written documentation was often scarce, and people with some means could re-invent themselves by traveling far enough away from any place they were known, there was real concern about dealing with discovered defects in the sacraments.

The outcome in teaching was the concept of a conditional sacrament. The Baptism, or Confirmation, or Ordination would be performed again, as if it had not been effective the first time around, but understood as a remedy of a defect, not as a completely new sacrament. The intention was to fill in any missing pieces, correct any erroneous pieces, and fulfill the original intentionality of the sacrament. If in fact—but unknowable—the first time around the sacrament was valid, then the second instance was precautionary, but not sacramental. If the second time around the sacrament was the valid one, then the first time had been ineffectual.

I know this is cutting things very fine, but the point is critical to our understanding of what evolved next. In the Orthodox/Catholic Tradition, the only time one would conduct a conditional Baptism or Ordination was if there were a reasonable chance that the first Baptism/Ordination was not a valid sacrament. And so the second time through would typically be counted as the 'real' sacrament. The point being, only one or the other ritual could be considered the 'real' one, and because of real doubt, the second one was the one. The first one would be in effect crossed off the books as not being a sacrament.

Moreover, since the sacrament was considered indelible—able

to be bestowed only once—it was and is considered sacrilege to perform a sacrament of initiation more than once.

This view has been shared throughout the sacramental communions, though exercised in slightly different ways. Conditional sacraments are exercised both within a communion as a remediation for lapses in oversight; and between communions, such as when a Catholic priest converts to Orthodoxy and is conditionally baptized, confirmed, and ordained.

It is this latter tradition of re-ordaining and re-consecrating clergy when they move from one communion to another that has directly impacted ISM thinking and practice. We'll look at this in more detail in Chapter 6.

BREAKS IN THE LINE OF BISHOPS

There have been times when, due to war, plague, etc. that all the bishops of a particular jurisdiction have died before they were able to make successors. The most prominent and most often cited of these situations is the break in the Coptic Orthodox succession, where the last bishop died before consecrating a successor. A synod of presbyters (priests) convened and elected a new bishop from their number, and designated three priests to perform the ordination. The three priests then laid hands on the candidate, using the ritual for ordaining a bishop, and made a new bishop. From that point, the new bishop was again the only one allowed to ordain additional clergy and his successor.

We should note that Orthodox and Roman churches all recognize and accept the Coptic Orthodox Orders as valid and legitimate, in full light of this process. Incidentally, this is the precedent John Wesley invoked when he ordained priests and made "superintendents" (an English word for *episcopos*) for the American colonial Methodist communities. And once created, only the Superintendents were allowed to ordain new clergy.

As a side note, a truly fascinating solution to a break in the succession was that of the "Dead Hand" Ukrainians who applied the lifeless (though presumably still grace-filled) hand of the last dead bishop to his successor's head at the culmination of the ordination rite to ensure the continuity of the episcopal succession!

A BISHOP'S AUTHORITY

For every bishop in the One Holy Catholic and Apostolic Church (including Orthodox, Oriental Orthodox, Nestorian, Catholic, Old Catholic, Anglican, and some Lutheran bishops), there are two physical documents:

Succession—the proverbial "roll of bishops." A Church maintains the record of the making of all its bishops, and every bishop can demonstrate the conveyance of episcopal Orders back through time to the Apostles. This is effectively an *exclusive* record—being a member of a single thread of succession within one's tradition.

Authority—the commissioning to a jurisdiction. A Church determines the need for a bishop, and commissions the bishop for a specific work, granting him the authority to act as a bishop of the Church for this specific work. This is effectively an *inclusive* record—marking the bishop as an equal member of the universal college of bishops.

☙

The Sacrament of Orders gave the Bishops the *ability* to be bishops—via the empowerment of the Holy Spirit to lead the Body of Christ. Only the particular Tradition itself, through its synod of bishops, could grant a bishop the *authority* to lead a jurisdiction. Put another way, a new bishop had to receive both the sacramental empowerment, and the place to do the work of bishop. But the Augustinian view created a loophole, such that bishops, once made and authorized, could wander about and perform the work of the bishop whereever they found themselves. The empowerment was forever; authority was a more problematic thing.

In the earliest communities of Christians, authority was directly derived from the Elder's association as student of an Apostle, or student of a student of an Apostle. This developed into the Elder being in authority because the person was vouchsafed (by a regional synod of Elders) to be a true keeper and teacher of the Apostolic Tradition. And this Elder was typically raised up from within the local community he now led. These Elders led their own local communities; but other Elders were what today we would call "non-territorial" bishops—the wandering missionaries who set out to create communities of faithful.

We've seen in this chapter how for Orthodoxy, through Cyprian, a bishop's ability and authority to lead are synonymous, assuming the bishop continues to teach the received fullness of Christian Tradition. For the Catholic West, authority emerged as a clearly-assigned jurisdiction of governance.

The exit of the Church of England (Anglicans) and the Old Catholics from Rome did not change the rules of the game in the West—all three bodies continued the Augustinian model. And authority was assigned by the synod of bishops for specific jurisdictional/diocesan governance.

So ingrained is this necessary assignment of jurisdiction in the West that Roman bishops who have lost their dioceses through war, depopulation, etc. have been assigned to titular sees (dioceses without actual laity and clergy, and typically named for long dead diocesan seats in no-longer Christian regions), so that they may rightly continue to be bishops and have authority in synod.

This equation of granting authority with assigning to jurisdiction has been adopted in many quarters of the ISM without critical evaluation. We have lost—and have the opportunity to recover, the non-territorial models of earliest Christianity.

4. GAME CHANGERS

THE ROOT CHURCHES OF THE INDEPENDENT SACRAMENTAL MOVEMENT emerged out of an amazingly energetic and complex era, and must be understood in this light.

In this Chapter we begin to narrow our focus and discussion to "the West"—in particular the countries and cultures within the historic jurisdiction of the Patriarch of Rome. This is not only because the history and movements are better known—but because the Augustinian definition of episcopacy created a unique set of dynamics that have played out most overtly in the West.

In the West in the 1700s the Enlightenment was in full swing with its idolatry of the rational. Institutional churches had become thoroughly flattened into requisite facets of social interaction, stratified by social class, with rather lifeless liturgies. The United States was created; and on its heels France's own revolution rebirthed the nation as a Republic. The Anglican Communion was born; the Dutch Old Roman Catholics completed their split from Rome.

Into the 1800s, the Romantic Movement was born, in reaction to the perceived loss of heart, the lack of inspiration, the missing soul at the core of society and personal lives. Initiatic fraternities and Lodges were founded. For Christianity this was the time of the Second Great Awakening in America, whose ripples spread back to Europe. This was a grass roots movement, a reaction to the ascendency of the rational in the mainline churches in the previous century. Like the Romantic Movement, it focused on heart, feeling, and experience.

Hindu, Zen, and Sufi traditions first appeared in scholarly circles and made a sensation, quickly spreading to the literati. And out of this ferment, the taproots of the Neopagan and Neo-Druid movements were set, and Hermeticism and Christian esotericism saw a fresh revival.

The later 1800s were a time of amazing changes and struggles in the mainline sacramental churches. In the West, the Episcopal Church in the US experienced its first schism, with the birth of the Reformed Episcopal Church. The German and Swiss Old Catholics split from Rome and joined their Dutch confreres over Roman doctrinal changes. Within the Roman church, there were trends towards circling the wagons and exerting ever-tightening control over the faithful, and innovating (or clarifying, depending on your view) doctrinal positions, coming to a sharp focus in the First Vatican Council.

The Europeans' fraternal and secret lodges were coming under a barrage of attacks from the Roman Catholics and various state governments due primarily to the degree of secrecy with which the lodges conducted their affairs and preserved members' anonymity.

In the East, the native Orthodox communities were experiencing a renewed invasion by Protestant, Catholic, and Anglican missionaries, who arrived with cash and textbooks and competing plans to co-opt the local cultures. Running in unique juxtaposition to this, a number of Orthodox leaders aspired to re-plant and rejuvenate Orthodoxy in the West, and these visionary bishops sought ways to make this happen.

In both Europe and North America, a surprising number of new religious groups emerged, such as the Mormons and the various schools of the New Thought movement, with visionary leaders creating significant followings.

"Secular" scholarship that focused on the Bible, non-canonical scriptures, ancient Christian history, and the history of theology all rose to prominence as academic tools and methodologies emerged to engage Christianity in new and uncensored ways. Energizing this were the multiple discoveries of very ancient texts throughout the Near East.

This chapter can only examine the most relevant high points of all this ferment, to see how the general social and religious mood of the times created the perfect storm for the emergence of the Independent sacramental Churches. Each movement is deserving of much greater study.

ENDING ROME'S MONOPOLY OF THE WEST

The Patriarchs of Rome had enjoyed a virtual religious (and political) monopoly over Western Europe for over 1000 years. Then, beginning with the secession of the Church of England in the 1500s, the jurisdiction of the Roman Patriarchate experienced a number of fractures. The Lutherans, the Anglicans, the Old Catholics, and the waves of Protestant revolt all took their toll on even the illusion of a monolithic Catholic Europe. Two of these separations are presented here, as they have the most important impact on our discussion of episcopacy and Orders.

Rome vs. Utrecht. In 696 Utrecht became the Primatial See of Holland, when Pope Sergius consecrated St. Willibrord as bishop. This episcopal seat eventually became a Prince-Bishopric of the Holy Roman Empire until 1528, when Prince-Bishop Henry of Bavaria ceded the sovereignty to the Emperor Charles V. The Archbishop of Utrecht had secured a number of unique rights for the Dutch Church, which allowed them to conduct ecclesiastical matters with a great deal of freedom from Rome. Over time, Rome looked for opportunities to reverse this situation.

In 1702, the Roman Catholic Church in Holland (comprising the Archiepiscopal See of Utrecht and the Bishoprics of Haarlem and Deventer) became separated from the rest of the Roman Church when Pope Clement XI suspended the Archbishop, Peter

Codde, resulting from political intrigue. The Dutch Church had chosen to harbor Jansenist refugees from Rome, and dared to oppose the Jesuits.

After the death of Archbishop Codde, Dominique Marie Varlet, missionary Roman Catholic Bishop of Babylon, acting without permission from Rome, restored the apostolic succession. In the 1730s the Dutch Church became the Old Roman Catholic Church, to distinguish it from those who adhered to a new hierarchy imposed on Holland by the Roman Church.

The Vatican Council of 1870 is a dividing line in the history of the Western church. Vatican I introduced the dogma of Papal Infallibility. From points all across Europe otherwise faithful Roman Catholics now found themselves at odds with their Church, and a surprising number turned to the Old Roman Catholic Church for Holy Orders for their clergy, and priests for their parishes. Those Catholics who departed the Roman Church over this dogma became known as Old Catholics, and many of their churches came together with the Dutch Church in the Union of Utrecht.

This lively confederation of national bodies in continental Europe (formerly extending to the Polish National Catholic Church in the US) has thrived down to the present, and would make possible a major source of ISM episcopal orders through the Old Catholics in England and the US, the Liberal Catholic bodies, and the Mariavite bodies.

Rome vs. Canterbury. The withdrawal of the Church of England from the Roman communion and the banishing of the Roman faith from British shores in the 1500s had created ecclesial bad blood between Canterbury and Rome that slowly simmered down through the years.

Vatican I and the Old Catholic separation fanned the flames of a Roman desire to re-exert monolithic religious control of Europe. In 1896 the Roman Church escalated an unseemly and baseless fight with the Church of England about whether or not Anglican Orders were indeed valid. Pope Leo XIII issued the papal bull *Apostolicae Curae*, which declared all Anglican orders "absolutely null and utterly void."

Coming at precisely the time when the Anglican world was being swept with the rise of the Anglo-Catholic movement (a return to its apostolic roots and practices, and a considered de-emphasis of its Reformation features), this was a blow to the Church of England. The Anglican Archbishops were quick to respond (in equally good Latin) with *Saepius Officio: Answer of the Archbishops of Canterbury and York to the Bull Apostolicae Curae of H. H. Leo XIII*.

The Anglican archbishops demonstrated in their response that Anglican Orders are valid and conform unambiguously to Augustinian criteria. Indeed, most major Orthodox bodies—and even some dissenters within Roman ranks—have expressed their opinion, based on their own study of the facts, that Anglican Orders are indeed valid, on equal footing with Roman, Old Catholic, and Orthodox Orders.

Yet the seed was planted. An unknown number of Anglican clergy and bishops secretly obtained re-ordination and re-consecration at the hands of Roman, Lutheran, Old Catholic, or Orthodox bishops.

Also at this time, as part of the development of Anglo-Catholic thinking, the Anglicans began to put forth their Three Branch theory, that the original Universal Catholic and Apostolic Church had three co-equal fraternal branches: the Eastern Orthodox, the Roman Catholic, and the Anglican. While neither the Romans nor the Orthodox were impressed by the logic, the Anglicans argued that in the Great Schism of 1054, the English Church was not involved, and had never separated from Orthodoxy.

This anxiety about the validity of Orders by Anglicans reached a high point at the turn of the 1900s, and continues to simmer even today thanks to repeated gratuitous Roman pronouncements on the subject. This anxiety about validity ripples out to the non-Canterbury Anglican bodies as well and will come to be an essential focus among ISM clergy.

Orthodoxy Returns to the West. While the Patriarch of Rome was sparring with his Anglican and Old Catholic confreres, several Orthodox prelates began to see in the West a field ripe for replanting the Orthodox faith. A small but crucial number of these prelates took innovative steps to sow Orthodox seeds.

Patriarch of the Syrian Orthodox Church of Antioch. In the 1860s, the Syrian Orthodox Church was led by Moran Mar Ighnatiyus Ya'qub II (Ignatius Jacob II), Patriarch of Antioch and of All the Domain of the Apostolic Throne. Mar Ya'qub became convinced that he could be instrumental in returning Orthodoxy to the West to those places where it had long since vanished. Mar Ya'qub would instill this openness to a restoration of Orthodoxy in the West into his bishops.

Mar Ya'qub's first effort at refounding a Western Orthodoxy came in the form of his authorization of the consecration in 1866 of the French Roman Catholic priest Jules Ferrette as an Orthodox bishop at the hands of the Syrian Metropolitan of Emesa, Mar Ighnatiyus Butrus IV al-Ma'usili (the future Patriarch Peter III). Ferrette was commissioned to found a mission in Western Europe, and made his way to Britain, where he became Bishop of Iona. Ferrette raised Richard Williams Morgan, an Anglican priest, to the episcopacy in 1874 and installed him as the first Patriarch of a restored Ancient British Church. Morgan's line from Ferrette passed into the majority of ISM bishops through Leon Checkemian and his successors.

Mar Butrus IV (Peter III), as Patriarch, authorized the consecration of French Old Catholic priest Joseph Rene Vilatte to the episcopacy in 1892 at the hands of the Malankaran Archbishop of Ceylon, Goa and India, Antonio Francisco Alvares (himself in Mar Butrus' succession). Vilatte had a thriving network of parishes in the upper Midwest of the United States, and his episcopacy brought cohesion to his work. Vilatte is one of the major source bishops for ISM orders worldwide.

Decades later, the Syrians would protest that no true ordinations of Western clergy had taken place. From an outsider vantage, these protests seem to result from political pressure from Western jurisdictions, as well as some consternation about the resulting careers of some of Vilatte's and Ferrette's successors. Yet detailed authentic documentation and first-person eyewitness accounts bear unambiguous witness to the facts of the ordinations.

Metropolitan of India, Assyrian Church of the East. Ulric Herford, an English Unitarian minister, determined to align himself with the Church of the East, which was then in Britain recently discovered and understood to preserve an ancient, un-Roman, and pristine form of Christian practice. To this end, he applied to the Metropolitan of India, Luis Mariano Soares for ordination, and in 1902 was raised by Soares to the episcopacy. Soares was pleased to be able to extend the jurisdiction of his Church into the West. Herford was made Bishop of Mercia and Middlesex with full jurisdiction over Great Britain and Ireland for the Church of the East. He was active among the English Old Catholics and networked with many in the ISM movements.

Orthodoxy in the America context. Historically, jurisdictions of the Patriarchates did not overlap. Order was preserved throughout the Eastern Christian world by clear agreements on which Patriarch provided pastoral and administrative oversight of which peoples and regions. A church might change its allegiance and form a union with a new Patriarch, but multiple patriarchates never shared overlapping oversight of the same people.

The United States in the 1800s was a new situation for the Orthodox world. For the first time large numbers of ethnic Orthodox lived together—Syrian, Greek, Russian, and Armenian, side by side by side by side. Historical precedent dictated that the first Orthodox Church to enter unclaimed territory would 'own' the jurisdiction of the people there. By this precedent, the Russian Orthodox were easily the first, having established outposts in Alaska and California very early on. However, in the US, the people to be served were already Orthodox, and looked for priests who provided their own liturgy in their own language.

Complicating this situation was the position of the Episcopal Church, which considered itself to be the presence of English-speaking Orthodoxy in America, an expression of Anglicanism's Three Branch Theory. During this period, the Episcopal Church took over pastoral oversight of the Romanian Orthodox Church briefly in 1923, and provided financial support for (and provided ethnic clergy for) the Syrian Orthodox immigrants.

Into this situation Aftimios Ofiesh, a Syrian Orthodox priest appeared. He applied to come to New York to minister to the faithful, and was consecrated a bishop for the Russian Orthodox Church, and made Archbishop of Brooklyn, of the Holy Eastern Orthodox Catholic and Apostolic Church of North America. This was to be the first English-speaking Orthodox jurisdiction. Ofiesh's mission was to unite the Orthodox faithful in a non-ethnic, English speaking church.

With the ethnic Orthodox clamoring for their own liturgy, spoken in their own languages, and the Episcopal Church pressuring Orthodox leadership, Ofiesh had a difficult road. Then the Syrian Orthodox Church sent in their own leadership (with the financial backing of the Episcopal Church)—a clear violation of territory. In 1929, the Russian Metropolitan Platon withdrew support for Ofiesh's church, and Ofiesh and his supporters voted to continue autonomously. Archbishop Ofiesh established the first non-ethnic Orthodox jurisdiction on American soil. He also would become a major source of ISM orders.

Russian Orthodoxy and the Revolution. The Russian Revolution, and the massive social, political, and economic upheavals visited on the Russian people created multiple competing divisions among the Orthodox faithful. Russia—a medieval rural country for centuries under the domination of a monarchy completely entwined with Orthodoxy—suddenly gave way to the Soviet Union as an officially atheist bureaucracy.

Some Orthodox leaders advocated an active accommodation to the new Soviet State; some Orthodox leaders advocated a total opposition to and separation from all political life; and some Orthodox leaders claimed various positions of compromise between the extremes. Complicating this was the attempt on the part of Orthodox leaders to provide meaningful support to the Russian faithful living on the North American continent.

A number of Russian bishops from various groups began to act independently of the Russian Synod and make new clergy and bishops to meet the pastoral needs of their North American flocks.

We find Russian bishops participating in 1927 with Aftimios Ofiesh to make bishops for Ofiesh's Orthodox Church in

America. We learn about the touching story of the American Henry Kleefisch, who in 1918 found himself sharing a Soviet prison cell with Orthodox prelates, and was consecrated by Metropolitan Sergij Stragorodskij in the future Patriarch's prison cell, to preserve the line of succession from extinction by the Soviets. In the mid-1950s John Fedtschenkov, American Exarch of the Russian Orthodox Church, participated with other ethnic Orthodox bishops in helping found new indigenous American missions. And most notably Joseph Klimovicz of the Russian Living Church in the 1940s and 1950s participating in making a number of Orthodox bishops for new indigenous American missions. All of these efforts rapidly jumped to ISM jurisdictions.

HUNGER FOR INITIATION

As a powerful expression of the Romantic Movement, the secret Lodges in the 1800s fully embraced the dynamic of Initiation into Mysteries. Lodges developed coherent systems of initiations, with lesser and greater Mysteries, full sacred theatrical rituals and vestments, and a rich mythic language. These Lodges were everything that was missing in the 'high and dry' socially correct institutional church options available at the time.

One could belong to more than one Lodge, and one's attainment could be recognized by another Lodge of similar outlook. Initiation into one Lodge tradition did not preclude initiation into another, and by the 1800s, there was a discernable sense that higher attainment was shown by having more than one Lodge's initiation under one's belt.

It is noteworthy that the guild of Freemasons during this period evolved into one of the cornerstones of the Lodge system, and in some ways, set standards for inclusivity of membership that crossed social class lines, based instead on shared interests and goals. Lodge membership crossed social class lines with more ease than was acceptable in the churches. And Lodges gave members an experiential and robust sense of a deeper visceral and mystical meaning of life—a vision of grand possibility and empowerment.

As we shall see in the next chapter, it is not surprising that the

Independent bishops who have been most instrumental in evolving the concept of episcopal lineage were the very same men who were most active in this Lodge tradition. And the wide spectrum of approaches of these bishops should also not surprise us. Men and women joined the Lodge system for a variety of reasons, ranging from a Traditionalist instinct that found refuge from the arid world of modernity; to esotericists and ritual magicians who found even deeper meanings in the Lodge rituals and myth; to Romantics who found in the Lodge rituals the very sacramental experience of daily life they were lacking from the churches; to modernists, who felt that it was time to replace the old myths of institutional Christianity.

One last thing to understand: in the ancient Mysteries and solid Lodge traditions, a person was not initiated until they had completed a substantive program of training and experiential learning. Both the ancient Mysteries and Lodge systems understood that crossing the threshold to deeper understanding meant encountering real spiritual energy, something akin to standing closer to the fire. Our ancient Christian ancestors also knew this, even to the point of not allowing Christians-in-training to see the ritual of the Lord's Supper. They knew that the Christian Mysteries, no less than the pagan Mysteries, were life-transforming thresholds, milestones on the journey home, and the process of becoming christed.

Sadly, in recent centuries, and especially since the reign of the rational, the Churches by and large have lost sight of the transformational power and grace-filled efficacy of the Mysteries we safeguard.

MELCHIZEDEK PRIESTHOOD

An outgrowth of the booming Lodge system was a re-appraisal of the biblical mentions of the Melchizedek Priesthood, also called the Order of Melchizedek. Melchizedek, a mysterious figure contemporary with Abraham, was a priest-king of "God Most High" (Gen. 14:18), who offered sacrifice of bread and wine (instead of the typical animal sacrifices of the early Israelites). His priesthood pre-dates that of the priesthood assigned to the

Levites at Mount Sinai by a couple of generations, and is notable for the lack of animal sacrifice. The Kabbalah sometimes considers Melchizedek to be the bearer of the hidden tradition, passing this on to Abraham during this ceremony of offering.

The first Christians understood the references to a successor to Melchizedek in Psalm 110 to point directly to Jesus, and this theme is explored in detail in the Epistle to the Hebrews. This is the origin of the theme of Jesus as "our great high priest."

Melchizedek presented a perfect figure from which to claim a separate and evocative priestly empowerment. Coming in prior to Christian priesthood, the Melchizedek priesthood allowed for access to a more primal spiritual energy, untouched by the Church. And since there was no record of a formal succession of this priesthood, it was a simpler matter to claim spiritual succession into this priesthood.

Alongside the re-enactment of Roman and Egyptian mystery priesthoods in the Lodge and magical systems, the Melchizedek priesthood also provided an enriching context. And with the rise of new religious movements, particularly in North America, the priesthood via Melchizedek found a lively new life in Latter Day Saints (Mormon), and various New Age beliefs.

NEW SPIRITUAL MOVEMENTS

The 1700s and 1800s were a time of astonishing breadth and richness of new religious movements. As a result of the Protestant Reformation and the rise of the rational method and the push-back of the Romantic movements, new groups, communities, and teachings sprang up all over Western Europe and America. While a lot of these movements followed the path of the Reformation by rejecting sacramental priesthood and ecclesiology, a smaller number continued to embrace the sacramental path, but found new ways of experiencing this way of doing church. We'll look at two significant movements as emblematic of the larger movement.

Doinel and the French Gnostics. The Eglise Gnostique was inaugurated as the result of a series of spirit communications received by Jules Doinel in 1888. He contacted discarnate Bogomil bishops, who commissioned him to restore the Gnostic

Church. During these communications, Doinel was spiritually consecrated "Bishop of Montsegur and Primate of the Albigenses" at the hands of the "Eon Jesus" and two Bogomil bishops.

Doinel, a librarian and an antiquarian of note, thoroughly researched the Cathar roots of his refounded Church (and their Gnostic predecessors), and imbued the Eglise Gnostique with Cathar doctrine and liturgical structure.

Doinel's Church was formed in a matrix of tremendous esoteric ferment on the Continent. Doinel's consecration set in motion several interwoven lineages of Gnostic jurisdictions and bishops; and his example of spiritual consecration was echoed in several other esoteric bishops emerging with their own traditions.

Almost from the beginning, Doinel's church and its successors were allied in various ways with the nascent Martinist (and other initiatic) movements. At various points, Doinel's church (and its successors) was infused with apostolic succession from the Syrian Gallican Church (of the Vilatte succession via Houssay's Gallican Church). This was valued as augmenting the spiritual lineage.

Church of Jesus Christ of Latter Day Saints (Mormons). In May—June 1829, the Prophet Joseph Smith, along with Oliver Cowdery, were ordained into the restored Aaronic and Melchizedeck priesthoods, on the banks of the Susquehanna River. This occurred during a period in which Smith and his trusted senior followers were in the midst of translating the newly-received Book of Mormon. Through this dual ordination, the two directly received a restored Old Covenant (culminating in the John the Baptist) and New Covenant (passing from Melchizedek down to Christ) priesthood.

Details concerning the date(s) and circumstances of the ordinations are hotly disputed, even among Mormons. Smith and Cowdery themselves wrote conflicting reports of the events, and changed their stories over time (though some speculate they were under vows to keep the whole of the story secret at the time). Further, it was not until after 1835 that missionaries of the LDS Church claimed specific restoration from Peter, James, and John. However, the core fact of a transmission and restoration of an authoritative priesthood for the Latter Day Saints is not in doubt.

Accounts vary as to whether the Aaronic priesthood was conveyed "by an angel" or by "John the Baptist." Likewise, accounts vary as to whether the Melchizedek priesthood was conveyed "by an angel" or by the apostles "Peter, James, and John." Whatever the facts, both priesthoods were safeguarded by direct tactile succession within the Church.

DARING TO THINK AND QUESTION

In the background of the movements in this chapter has been a two-fold revolution of thought: the critical re-appraisal of history and tradition, and the critical re-appraisal of Christian scripture.

The profession of historian was coming into being at the time, alongside the other new professions of archeologist, anthropologist, and psychologist. The "hard" sciences of physics, biology, and physiology were experiencing revolutions in perspective and technique. The empirical method of the sciences was adopted wholesale into the humanities. For the first time, this empirical methodology caused the new historians to grapple with the discovery that written history, up to the time of the Enlightenment, had no notion of objective, unbiased reportage. The maxim "history is written by the victors" encapsulated the emerging understanding that all records of human events have a point of view (or an ax to grind!). And so a new project in the discipline of history was to figure out—with the aid of archeology, anthropology, and textual studies—how to separate "fact" (inasmuch as any could be determined) from "truth."

The study of ancient texts—both the writing and the physical record (papyrus scrolls, clay tablets, and later bound books)—arose as a critical discipline within archeology. Scholars studied and began to unlock the ancient written languages.

It was inevitable that this skill and method of inquiry would be directed to study the biblical texts and record. Scholars compared the biblical stories of the Israelites and our earliest spiritual ancestors to the physical record of the civilizations and settlements of Palestine, Egypt, Sumeria. It was perhaps the archeological discovery that the Earth is millions of years old (while the Bible chronology considered the Earth to be about 5000 years old) that began to give scholars a solid foundation for inquiry. If the book of Genesis were not literally true as a history of the physical world, what did this mean? Scholars began to look at the genres of story-telling in the Bible, unwittingly rediscovering what the earliest Christian theologians already knew: the Bible was part allegory, part myth, part parable, part polemic, and all telling the faith understandings of its many writers and editors. How could a person approach the many texts stitched together into the Christian Bible, and recognize how to read each text?

Shaking the faithful scholars and the churches alike were the discoveries beginning in the late 1800s of the many other non-canonical texts of the earliest Christian communities—the writings that did not make it into the Christian Bible as we have it today. These earliest fragmentary discoveries (it would be another 50 years before the Dead Sea Scrolls and the Nag Hammadi Library would be found) raised tantalizing hints that Christianity was much more diverse in its roots than anyone previously thought—and that the Church's self-understanding as a single stalk sprung directly from a homogenous teaching of the Apostles was not factual.

We are still living today with the shock waves resulting from these first inquiries, and subsequent scholarship. On the one hand, this scholarship and inquiry has shaken the foundations of assumptions about the faith. On the other hand, this scholarship gave people awareness and access to the separate strands of Christian Tradition (the several flavors of Oriental Orthodoxy, the variations in Chalcedonian Orthodoxy, the non-Latin jurisdictions that sheltered under the administration of Rome, etc.) and the many now-lost strands of the early faith (the Ebionites, the Valentinians, the Thomasines, the Sethians, etc.).

It was this permission to dare to ask questions and think differently about our faith history that contributed to the dynamism of the ISM bishops, as we will see in the next section.

EPISCOPAL SUCCESSION AND LINEAGE

"Dorian Herbert...[has been] conditionally re-consecrated...by de Willmott Newman of the Ferrette succession. There is perhaps no need to point out the grave theological fallacy implicit in such a performance, grounded, presumably, on a confusion between the powers conferred by consecration and those conferred by jurisdiction." *p.38*

"[De Willmott Newman] is not now in communion with Crow, but he claims to have received into union with himself a number of other *episcopi vagantes*, to whom he has given conditional re-consecration, and then himself received consecration from them with a view to "combining the lines of succession" under the apparent misconception that a person is consecrated a bishop of a particular line of succession rather than a bishop of the Church of God." *p. 51, note 1*

—*Henry R. T. Brandreth,* EPISCOPI VAGANTES AND THE ANGLICAN CHURCH

"What I believe we are seeing are the seeds of a new kind of ministry that can adapt itself to the time and place of its exercise, the needs of the moment, and the people who are actually present in that particular place at that particular time. And yet is it so new? Is it not perhaps the very way that St. Paul set about spreading the Gospel and building the Church? Speaking as a Jew to the Jews, a Greek to the Greeks? Respecting the customs and ethos of the local people rather than seeking to impose his personal will upon them? And yet he brought them the same Lord, the same Christ, the same Holy Spirit, and the same Gospel." *p. 16*

—*Alan Bain,* BISHOPS IRREGULAR, AN INTERNATIONAL DIRECTORY OF INDEPENDENT BISHOPS

5. DISCOVERING LINEAGE

AS WE'VE SEEN, FROM THE VERY BEGINNING Christianity has had an implicit sense of lineage. Originally this was a person-to-person lineage of teaching from a specific apostle, or the claim to an apostolic founder for one's church community.

With the imposition of the Imperial Church by Constantine and the orthodox bishops, the Church gained a new, more universal perspective, and local or regional lines of tradition were subsumed in this larger vision. But the local and regional traditions and practices did not disappear. With deeper roots than the Imperial mandate, these regional differences remained, understood and cherished as the specific flavors of their apostolic founders. Even as in later centuries in the West the Popes began to methodically suppress local variation in the name of a monolithic faith and obedience, local traditions found new ways to live on and express themselves.

In short: there have always been distinct strands of what we conveniently consider a single Christian Tradition. We must be honest about the multiplicity of Christian Traditions if we're going to fully understand what the Independent Sacramental Movement makes explicit in the concept of Lineage.

A NEW UNDERSTANDING OF SUCCESSION AS LINEAGE

From the point of view of traditionalists and mainline jurisdictions, any discussion of lineage is misguided at best. As we saw in chapter 3, since the time of Cyprian and Augustine a bishop is only possible as a direct lineal descendent from his predecessor in office, and only possible as a replacement for a diocesan vacancy. (We'll set aside any discussion of the use of missionary dioceses and titular dioceses.) The notion that one might make a bishop for a new jurisdiction, or for a new church, had been lost 1500 years previously.

In the opening decades of the 20th entury, ISM bishops followed the standard Augustinian or Cyprianic rules of the road for bishops. Those few bishops who were conditionally consecrated had actual concerns about the validity of their original consecrations, and viewed the conditional event as their actual Sacrament of Orders.

Yet in these same early decades, something new emerged in the teaching of the Tradition: some Independent bishops who had been conditionally ordained began to count both ordinations and to claim the lineage/tradition from both events as "real." This does not seem to have been an intentional strategy or coordinated effort to create something new. It naturally arose as, for example, a bishop was first ordained by a bishop in the Syrian Orthodox succession, and later was conditionally consecrated by a bishop in the Old Catholic succession. At some point, a few pioneering bishops began to embrace, for example, both traditions as informing their own episcopacies.

Some of these bishops began to articulate aspirations of reuniting the various threads of Christian Tradition into a single Body once more; a few others had arguably less noble aspirations. They laid out a strategy of receiving multiple conditional ordinations as a way of reuniting in themselves the many strands of Tradition, by counting both their original ordination as Bishop, and the additional conditional ordinations as Bishop. This was a new thing, and a practice without solid ecclesial theory behind it.

Then in the 1940s a number of ISM bishops went a step further with the idea to "strengthen" their lines (remember in the West, non-Roman bishops still were prone to anxiety about the validity of their consecrations)—not because they doubted that the original ordination was defective, but because they believed they could increase their overall validity by increasing the number of threads of Tradition, the number of lines of episcopacy.

This was a true innovation: the exchange of consecrations. In this ritual, the form of the ordination of a bishop was and is followed, but the intention and action focuses on each participating bishop passing his/her lines to the others, by laying on of hands. Sometimes this would simply consist of a bishop passing on his lines to another bishop who desired to increase his own. Sometimes this looked like a round-robin of sub-conditional ordinations. Sometimes this looked like a circle of original ordinations. The Augustinian rules of validity are by definition violated—or at least suspended—since each bishop had already been validly ordained to the episcopate previously.

And when they themselves made new bishops, they commonly considered that the fullness of their accumulated lines was passed on to the new bishop.

The core of this phenomenon emerged first in Great Britain, and flourished side by side with the Anglican Orders controversy still simmering with Rome. Anglican clergy were sneaking off to be re-ordained and re-consecrated at the hands of sympathetic Roman, Lutheran, Old Catholic, and Orthodox bishops in unknown numbers. And Anglican clergy were also quietly becoming members of various ISM churches, some functioning as priests in their Anglican parishes, and simultaneously functioning as ISM bishops. For example, Percy Dearmer continued to exercise his ministry as a priest within the Church of England, even writing a landmark book on proper Anglo-Catholic ritual practices; yet he was also an ISM bishop, receiving episcopacy into the English Old Catholic line of Mathew. And Richard Williams Morgan was also an Anglican vicar, while also a leader of the Druid revival, and first Patriarch of the Ancient British Church, receiving episcopal Orders from Jules Ferrette (Syrian Orthodox origins). In this heady mix of anxiety, ISM bishops began to talk about receiving particular episcopal lines of succession. Bishops began creating new churches from the top down—unconsciously rediscovering the most ancient model of wandering missionary bishops.

For those charting an Independent Orthodox course in the West, the challenge was greater: how to adhere to the Cyprianic definition of Church and Orders—there is no grace outside the body of mutually recognized Orthodox jurisdictions (and so, no valid clergy)—yet receive episcopacy and function under frankly Augustinian circumstances.

These pioneering Independent bishops rediscovered something valuable: that alongside the Sacrament of Orders (the threshold of initiation into priesthood and episcopacy) there was the possibility of initiation into threads of Tradition (Western, Chalcedonian, Oriental Orthodox, etc.). In addition to the universal single College of Bishops that constituted the Mystical Body of Christ, there were smaller synods of bishops of various threads of Tradition.

These ISM bishops were, in truth, making explicit something that each thread of Tradition had practiced for centuries. Rome has long required any Anglican priest or bishop (and on occasion Orthodox clergy) who converts to Catholicism to be re-ordained (conditionally). Orthodox traditions have usually required Catholic or Anglican clergy to be re-baptized, re-confirmed, and re-ordained, though have at times welcomed clergy via economia (acknowledging their Orders as valid). Anglicans have tended to be more gracious about recognizing Catholic or Orthodox sacraments as valid, though have also at times required re-ordination.

Historical practice has testified to what the Tradition has been mute about; that each thread of the Tradition has its own lineage, and in practice one must be initiated into that thread. The only ISM innovation was the conscious decision to retain the original as well as the new threads of Tradition, now plaited together into a single, stronger, and broader strand.

THE LODGE FACTOR

I believe we cannot fully appreciate the innovation and context of Lineage for ISM bishops without recognizing the cultural background of the fraternal and occult Lodges. To my mind the entire concept of Lineage exchanges and gathering would not have even arisen were it not for the unique constellation of people who became Independent bishops at this time.

A surprisingly large number of our ISM bishop forebears were involved in secret societies, Masonic organizations, initiatic orders, and other esoteric movements. Just a small sampling of bishops who stand in most of our ISM lines of succession includes: Masons (J.S.M. Ward, Hugh George de Willmott Newman, Herbert Monzani-Heard), Liberal Catholics/Theosophists (James Wedgwood, Charles Leadbeater), Martinists/French Gnostics (Jules Doinel, Jean Bricaud), Rosicrucians (George Plummer, Stanislas De Witow/Witowski), Spiritualists (Charles Boltwood), English Gnostics (Richard, duc de Palatine), Ritual Mages (Bernard Crow), Druidic revival (Richard Williams Morgan).

It was common at this time for initiates of equal seniority or leadership stature in various Lodge Traditions to grant each other status and standing in their own Lodge Tradition. So a Scottish Rite Mason and a York Rite Mason of equivalent rank might grant each other status—exchange initiations—so that both now shared each line of Tradition. These pioneering ISM bishops had re-discovered the initiatic origins of the ordination rite. While a particular initiation can be undertaken only once, the Initiatic path is inclusive, not exclusive. One can undertake more than one initiatic path, and it was held that to do so enriches the person.

The fact of esoteric involvement by these bishops is not surprisingly omitted from many contemporary ISM bishops' records, as this is something of an embarrassment to many current heirs of those bishops. Even bishops of the most Orthodox or Roman traditions were active Lodge members, and one need not search very hard at all to discover this.

But esoteric involvements aside, there are several lineages that are openly esoteric, and counted among the lines to be gathered by ISM bishops. The most prolific of these lineages originated with Jules Doinel and the Eglise Gnostique and its various permutations, and his successor Jean Bricaud (who was the first to combine Doinel's line with the apostolic line of Vilatte). Lines also originated with Richard, the duc de Palatine and the Ecclesia Gnostica and the offshoots of the English Gnostic tradition. Other lines of Inner Priesthood also derive from W. G. Gray, Rosamonde Miller, Dion Fortune, and Rudolph Steiner.

The Liberal Catholic Church is a unique lineage in this group: it had arisen out of the Old Catholic Church mission in Great Britain, changing its name and objectives—but always holding the apostolic succession alongside it's more esoteric features.

It is an interesting irony that completely non-esoteric bishops will trace their line back to Vilatte through Bricaud and the French Gnostics, or claim the Ferrette line back through the duc de Palatine, or claim the Mathew line through Leadbeater or Wedgwood.

It is likewise interesting that these non-apostolic lines have taken on the conventions of apostolic transmission. Perhaps because of the commingling of the apostolic succession from Vilatte with the spiritual succession from Doinel, it has become important to maintain the conventions of valid succession.

NAMING THE LINEAGES IN PLAY

One of my favorite bishop friends sees the ISM bishops' fascination with lineage as a special form of stamp collecting. And in listening to the episcopal one-up-man-ship over the years, I tend to agree. There is something about the mania to collect lineages that reduces the whole matter to avarice and envy, greed and ego. Some lines are shared by virtually all bishops; others are quite "rare," and highly prized in some quarters.

But the point must be made: we cannot know what lines we have unless we have a standard measure of what lines of tradition are in play. And as you might expect, there is no one single list.

In the mid-20th century, a general agreement coalesced among the Independent bishops that there were 16 known lines of apostolic succession (that were available through transmission into the Independent movement). Hugh George de Willmott Newman, Mar Georgius I, Patriarch of Glastonbury and Catholicos of the West is perhaps the best known in this effort to name and gather lines of succession. By 1956, through *sub conditione* consecrations and what we now call exchanges of lines, it was believed that he had accumulated all sixteen lines (though a few of these lines cannot have been conveyed as we'll see in Chapter 8). A quick scan will reveal the somewhat contrived nature of the list when compared to actual source traditions of apostolic succession:

Anglican
Non-Juring (Anglican)
Old Catholic
Liberal Catholic
Mariavite Catholic
Order of Corporate Reunion
Russian Orthodox
Russo-Syrian Orthodox
Syrian Antiochene
Syrian Malabar
Syrian Gallican
Syro-Chaldean
Coptic Orthodox
Greek Melkite
Chaldean Uniate
Armenian Uniate

By the end of the 20th century, the list of lines of succession to be acquired had (debatably) grown from de Willmott Newman's 16, to upwards of 22, depending on how one counts (and probably by how many lines one has accumulated). Keizer lists 22 lines, though this list, like Newman's, 1) does not reflect all the lines from the Eastern Churches; 2) conflates some unique lineages under a single heading; and 3) also includes some lines that cannot have been conveyed (see Chapter 8). Keizer's list provides the following six lines as additions to de Willmott Newman's above:

Anglican-Celtic
Roman Catholic
Orthodox Patriarchate—Constantinople
Coptic Uniate
Templar
Gnostic

Both lists neglect a simpler and more accurate perspective: that all apostolic lines ultimately derive from the Apostles, commissioned by Christ Jesus.

GATHERING LINEAGES

Now that we know *that* we can collect lines, and we know *what* lines are available, how do we do it?

There are three distinct ways that bishops claim to collect lines: one or more sub-conditional ordinations; mutual exchanges of consecrations; and to a much lesser extent economia. The ISM has tended to use all three of these interchangeably to collect lineages. There is a tacit assumption in all the discussion of lineage collection through the decades that lineage is conferred the same way as the Sacrament of Orders: through laying on of hands, during public celebration of Eucharist, etc.

Conditional ordination, as we saw in chapter 3, was and is the means to correct a known or suspected defect in the original sacrament. As we discussed, a person's ordination is then counted only from this second event. By the implicit logic, if the first sacrament is invalid, one should not be able to receive any sort of lineage from it. One cannot begin to add lineages until after the sacrament has been conferred.

Economia is the agreement by which a non-Orthodox clergy is received into Orthodoxy without having to undergo conditional (or original, from the Orthodox perspective) ordination. There is no actual laying on of hands, no sacrament being enacted. It is therefore doubtful whether we can or should count a new lineage here—presumably from the bishop primarily responsible for issuing the economia. It is included here since a number of bishops *do* count lineage as conveyed via economia.

The mutual exchange of lineage, or the additional consecration(s) to receive lineage, is the unambiguous—if historically unsupported—method for gaining lines.

Questions naturally arise out of this situation; you won't be surprised to learn that there is no consensus.

How do we sort out what consecrations were sacramental from those that were Lineage-related?

When we trace the actual thread of the Sacrament of Orders conveyed, do we trace only our primary consecrator, and his primary consecrator, and so on? Or do we include the co-consecrators?

When a bishop who has participated in exchanges of consecrations makes a new bishop, do the lines received by the exchange(s) pass on to the new bishop?

We'll try to sort these out in the next chapter.

6. CHARTING SUCCESSION AND LINEAGE: THE RULES OF THE ROAD

MUCH OF THIS CHAPTER IS DISTILLED from conversations with and observations of my fellow ISM bishops, reading a large number of their lineage documents, reading the available historical documents, and watching for the unspoken general rules already in play.

I began my episcopal life by adopting—as most of us do—the whole notion of lineage without reflecting on it, or knowing the context for it. I dutifully researched and pulled together my lineage document (150 pages worth, with two dozen charts—I'm a bit of an over-achiever), and spent many hours reflecting on the lineages, the traditions, and the work of my many predecessors.

But in my researches, I began to read more deeply on succession and authority, and on the reasoning of ISM bishops for collecting consecrations and lineages. I hit the major disconnect between the widely-accepted Western definition of validity and the use of lineages to "fix" this. I abandoned my whole lineage document, and created in its place a brief statement of my apostolic succession—the sacramental line from my consecrators through their consecrators. I counted from the conditional consecrations. I was a hard-nose about it.

But I kept reflecting, kept mulling over this whole luxuriant phenomenon of lineages. Was it possible that the Holy Spirit was involved somewhere in this whole thing? If so, how? What purpose does the aggregation of lineages serve that is not served by the bishop's ordination?

I believe the Holy Spirit *is* up to something in the ISM, up to something with the emerging concept of lineages. In this chapter, I will attempt to unfold this emerging concept—to point to where I see a grace-full thing happening, and to instigate a larger conversation.

☙

The concept of episcopal lineage as something explicit to be acquired or received, and charted and tracked and passed on, is unique to the ISM. Lineage has been used as a kind of shorthand for tradition. If apostolic succession is a symbol of the oneness of the faith received from the Apostles, then episcopal lineage is a symbol of the rich variety of the traditions that have evolved in Christian life. Lineage is about embracing the inevitable diversity of expressions of our human faith, held in a dynamic tension with the unity of the Body of Christ.

At its worst, the Independent world can rightly be accused of an embarrassing idolatry of episcopal lineages. Historical circumstance, a human need for respect—both as clergy and as churches—and the pervasive cultural angst over validity of our orders, are all focused sharply through the lens of Independent Sacramental life.

At its best, the Independent world can be honored for a courageous ecumenism of spirit and practice that seeks to recover and embrace the many theological, spiritual, and liturgical traditions of the past 2000 years. Life in the margins has revealed a freedom to seek out what was lost, and to respond to the Spirit's invitation to renew and renovate—to re-weave the frayed tapestry of Christian Tradition.

Based on historic sacramental practice and generations of ISM practice, I propose five basic rules for understanding and documenting how one's episcopal succession and lineage work:

Rule 1: A community determines the validity of its sacraments
Rule 2: A person becomes a bishop at the first valid ordination
Rule 3: Every bishop laying on hands ordains the bishop being made
Rule 4: Ordaining bishops convey all their lines to the new bishop
Rule 5: Bishops exchanging lines convey all their lines to each other

RULE 1: A COMMUNITY DETERMINES THE VALIDITY OF ITS SACRAMENTS

One of the enduring gifts of the Orthodox/Catholic synodal model of doing Church is the understanding that issues of validity of sacraments are properly the responsibility of the governing bishops of the jurisdiction. By convention and mutual respect, the various Patriarchates did not and do not question or intrude on these matters with their fellow Patriarchs. Of course, there was an awareness that sacraments might be celebrated with different nuances; but the responsibility to ensure the minimum requirements of validity were retained by the Patriarch or governing bishop of a jurisdiction.

As we've seen in Chapter 4, Rome broke this inter-jurisdictional covenant by openly and improperly challenging the validity of Anglican orders. It is interesting that a part of the response from Orthodox leaders (as well as the argument by the Anglican archbishops) was a focus on the inappropriateness of Rome's action, since such a determination was and is not theirs to make.

In the ISM, we are faced with the challenge to find historic precedents for vouchsafing the validity of bishops we raise up for existing as well as for new jurisdictions and missions, and the opportunity to listen to the Spirit leading us into new territory.

The bedrock principle remains: it is the responsibility of a jurisdiction to ensure its sacraments are properly conducted to conform to agreed practice of the universal Church. Whether a jurisdiction conforms its determination on the teachings of Cyprian or Augustine is for them to discern.

In the scope of our discussion, the question of validity of sacraments arises in three key circumstances:

New Christians are baptized and new clergy are ordained within an existing communion. This is the least controversial circumstance with the clearest delineation of responsibility. The bishops, clergy, and baptized members of a communion together own the responsibility to ensure that the sacraments are done properly and according to the teachings (Cyprianic or Augustinian) accepted by the communion. As long as everyone agrees, we may assume that all is proper. No person outside the communion has a legitimate voice in the discussion, unless specifically invited by the communion for the purpose of discernment.

Baptized Christians or ordained clergy move from one communion to another. When a Christian moves from communion A to communion B, it is only then that communion B becomes responsible to determine—for its own constituents—whether the new person's sacraments of initiation have been rightly performed and received, and only in terms of communion B. Note that communion B does not have the freedom here to openly comment on the validity of the sacraments of communion A as a whole (though this of course always hangs as a shadow over the deliberation); rather, it simply has responsibility to ensure that new members have received the sacraments of initiation in keeping with its own understanding.

New clergy are ordained for a new mission or ministry. Particularly in the ISM, clergy are regularly ordained with the understanding that they will not be affiliated with the jurisdictions of the ordaining bishops, but rather will be striking out on their own missions, fulfilling vocations to do a new thing. With no existing communion and no receiving communion to review or confirm the validity of the ordination, how are we to think about this?

In such circumstances (and my own ordination as bishop was such an event), it is the solemn responsibility of the ordaining bishops to ensure that the Sacrament of Initiation to the episcopacy is done in ways that conform to the understanding of validity amongst the ordaining bishops' own communions. In my example, the three ordaining bishops were all leaders in the Federation of St. Thomas Christians, and so their discernment of my appropriateness for ordination and their conduct of the Sacrament of Ordination conformed to their standards for validity.

In the common event that bishops from multiple jurisdictions gather to raise up a new bishop for a new mission, the bishops are responsible to confer and discern together, to ensure that the ordination of the new bishop conforms to their standards of validity. In this way, the ordaining bishops stand as proxies for the universal Church, and are accountable as such to any who would question the new bishop's orders. The responsibility for ISM bishops is clear and profound: when raising up a new bishop to go forth into new ministry to gather a community, the ordaining bishops must ensure that this new bishop is ordained according to the agreed practice of the universal Church (whether as framed by Cyprian or Augustine).

RULE 2: A PERSON BECOMES A BISHOP AT THE FIRST VALID ORDINATION

As we've discussed early on in this book, there is a general understanding that—as with all the sacraments of initiation—the act of ordination to the episcopacy creates an "imprint of character on the soul." It is a once-for-all sacrament, or in the traditional vocabulary, it is indelible.

Before the 1930s, identifying when the first valid ordination occurred was usually simple, since the vast majority of ISM bishops were ordained but once. It gets more confusing after this, when more bishops began undergoing multiple consecrations.

I take a common sense approach, based on observation. For ordinations up to about 1940, I look at the original and subsequent consecrations for a bishop, and look at the bishop's activities and affiliations before and after. In most cases, a bishop who received a second consecration devoted the rest of his life to the jurisdiction and tradition giving the second consecration. In these cases, it is relatively simple to decide that an actual *conditional* ordination has occurred, and the path of apostolic succession follows back from the conditional action, but not the original ordination (which was by definition thought to be in doubt for some reason).

From about the 1940s on, it is sometimes more difficult to determine the actual path of apostolic succession, because some bishops received multiple consecrations with no unequivocal sense of commitment to the last one received. When no certain event can be identified as the Sacrament of Orders, I recommend taking a conservative approach, and counting the original ordination as the apostolic path, and the subsequent events as opportunities to add and consolidate lines. While this is an imperfect solution, most of the bishops in question have passed on, and their papers do not record (or are not available for review) what their thinking was on the matter.

The textbook example of this approach is that of Hugh George de Willmott Newman, Mar Georgius.

Bishop Alan Stanford, on his apostle1.com website quotes an unnamed writer who reports on the work of Mar Georgius, and his pioneering intentional work of gathering conditional consecrations:

> *"Having undertaken the work of the restoration of the Orthodox Apostolic Catholicism of Undivided Christendom, he and those with him realized in the early days of his pontificate, that while all consecrations and ordinations of proven validity are equally efficacious irrespective of any particular line of Apostolic Succession; nevertheless, in the present divided state of Christendom, some degree of 'irregularity' must inevitably attach itself to acts lacking the ecumenical sanction of the One Body Mystical, being derived as they are from a part of the whole, it was felt under Divine guidance, that to remedy this position and also at the same time to counter any doubts which might be alleged, even though contrariness or ignorance against any particular lines of succession that the existing Orders of this Rite should be fortified by*

> *a series of conditional consecration have also the force of co-consecration and of additional commission in the ecumenical sense, thus bringing into being, an ECUMENICAL APOSTOLIC SUCCESSION derived from every part of The One Holy Catholic and Apostolic Church.*
>
> *"The action of Mar Georgius (and others) in receiving additional lines of succession has been the subject of certain criticism in more than one quarter. It is readily agreed that in a united Christendom such a thing would be both unnecessary and, indeed, wrong; for under those conditions consecration 'sub conditione' would be called for only when some specific doubt had arisen as to the validity of the original consecration. But, in a divided church, quite different considerations apply."*

As an illustration, following is the list of ordinations and consecrations received by de Willmott Newman. By our Rule, only the first consecration can be the Sacrament of Orders, and the one that counts as the event at which de Willmott Newman was actually made a bishop. The rest, by his own admission and intention, were consecrations to receive additional lineages. Following are the lineages received by de Willmott Newman from Maxey:

On 6 June 1946, Wallace David de Ortega Maxey and Hugh George de Willmott Newman (Mar Georgius) mutually exchanged lines of succession. Also exchanging lines with them at this time were: John Sebastian Marlow Ward, Richard Kenneth Hurgon, John Syer, Charles Leslie Saul, and Frank Ernest Langhelt. At this consecration, de Willmott Newman conveyed the following lineages to Maxey, et al: 10 April 1944, consecrated by William Bernard Crow (the Sacrament of Ordination for de Willmott Newman); 4 January 1945, consecrated s.c. by Sidney Ernest Page Needham; 29 April 1945, consecrated s.c. by Charles William Keller; 20 May 1945 exchanged consecrations with: Hedley Coward Bartlett, Francis Ernest Langhelt, George Henry Brook, and John Syer; 25 August 1945, consecrated s.c. by John Sebastian Marlow Ward; 6 June 1946, exchanged lines with Maxey, et al.

At this consecration, Maxey conveyed the following lineages to de Willmott Newman, et al: 2 January 1927, consecrated by William Montgomery Brown, assisted by William Henry Francis Brothers, Albert Jehan, and Josef Zielonka. 24 March 1927, consecrated s.c. by William Henry Francis Brothers, assisted by Josef Zielonka. 10 February 1929, consecrated s.c. by George Augustus Newmark, assisted by Edwin Wallace Hunter. 24 March 1929, consecrated s.c. by Edwin Wallace Hunter, assisted by Gregory Lines and Francis John Barwell Walker. 23 August 1945 exchanged consecrations with: Antoine Joseph Aneed, Charles H. Hampton, Henry Joseph Kleefisch, and Lowell Paul Wadle. 6 June 1946, exchanged lines with de Willmott Newman, et al.

I believe that Mar Georgius was on to something. Contrary to the unnamed writer quoted above however, I urge that we maintain the distinction between what is conveyed by the Sacrament of Ordination as a bishop, and what is conveyed through subsequent consecration into episcopal lineages.

RULE 3: EVERY BISHOP LAYING ON HANDS ORDAINS THE BISHOP BEING MADE

Once we've sorted out the actual ordination event in Rule 2, we move to this third Rule, which determines—when multiple bishops assisted in performing the Sacrament of Orders—how many of the bishops are said to pass along their own apostolic succession to the new bishop.

There are two preferences among ISM bishops of reckoning a bishop's sacramental line(s): the first focuses on the person of the "primary" ordaining bishop, and reckons that only the apostolic line held by the primary consecrator is passed to the new bishop. This approach describes a single chain of hands back through time. The second focuses on the whole group of the ordaining bishops, and reckons that the new bishop receives the lines of each bishop participating in the actual ordination of the new bishop. This approach describes something looking more like a family tree—that eventually narrows back down to the original apostolic sources.

And remember, at this point, we're still only looking at the path of sacramental transmission.

I suspect that the first preference above is an attempt to restrict claims made by new bishops, and generally confuses the issue of *authority* within a tradition (which we discussed in chapter 3), and the *ability* to be a bishop.

The second preference is more true to history and tradition and actual practice. After all, the reason that Orthodox and Catholic and Anglican bodies have traditionally required a minimum of three bishops to make a new bishop is to erase any doubt that the new bishop is rightly ordained. By having multiple bishops lay hands on the new bishop, the Church could be assured that any unknown defect in the succession would be covered—assuming at least one of the bishops had an undamaged (valid) line of succession. One would then necessarily need to pay attention to all the sacramental lines contributed, since any or all of them could be intact.

Beyond this, the symbol of many bishops making a new bishop is the reminder that the new bishop is made by, and enters into, the universal college of bishops. This is a beautiful and powerful symbol, revealing a much richer portion of the true original nature of the Order of Bishops.

I adopt the second view that each ordaining and assisting bishop necessarily contributes his or her apostolic lines to the new bishop. Each apostolic bishop traces the line of succession through all the bishops who laid on hands during the ordination.

RULE 4: ORDAINING BISHOPS CONVEY ALL THEIR LINES TO THE NEW BISHOP

Now that we have identified the transmission of the Sacrament of Orders, we cross into the more contentious matter of what else may be passed along during the ordination rite.

For a portion of the ISM world, only Rules 1 through 3 matter, and the concept of lineages is rejected outright as being foreign to the Tradition and teaching of orders. Their viewpoint and reasoning are soundly argued, and I respect their efforts to retain focus on the Sacrament of Orders.

And yet I am convinced there is more going on. I am convinced that when a new bishop is ordained and consecrated, s/he receives not only the fullness of the apostolic lines from each of the ordaining bishops; but also receives any episcopal lineages those ordaining bishops also hold, including any non-apostolic esoteric lines.

There are also two conventions for reckoning which lineages are passed: the first assumes that all lineages received by a bishop—through ordination and any subsequent consecrations—are inextricably woven together, and thus are passed as a set to any new bishop during ordination. The second convention assumes that a bishop can intentionally choose which specific lineages are to be passed to a new bishop during ordination. Some bishops in fact believe they can state and control which lineages they are conveying when they make a new bishop.

This belief in one's ability to select which lineages are passed is unique to the Independent movement, and I suggest that it highlights the basic confusion between the sacramental act of ordaining a bishop, with the matter of granting a new bishop authority and jurisdiction. What is really at stake often is simply blocking any potential claim that a newly-made bishop might make that s/he is now authorized to take a leadership position in one of her/his consecrator's jurisdictions by virtue of lineage received.

For example: a bishop colleague received her Sacrament of Orders within a unique esoteric Christic jurisdiction. Over the years, she has participated as assisting bishop in the consecration of other bishops, but has been at pains to claim that she is conveying only her apostolic lines, and not the unique esoteric lineage. Those who covet rare or especially difficult to obtain lines have nevertheless been able to show the links in the transmission between their own ordinations, and this bishop. I suspect that what is truly at stake for this bishop is to protect the esoteric tradition from any claimants by those in the succession. What would make the whole conversation moot is for all concerned to understand the great difference between ordination by bishops of a certain line of succession, and authority to participate in and lead a certain line of succession and tradition.

☙

When the notion of gathering and passing on multiple post-ordination lineages emerged in the first half of the 20th century, there were earnest questions about how this was to be done. Some bishops wondered if there should be a separate consecration liturgy for each line, and the liturgy done according to the tradition of the line passed. Common sense and simplicity won out (not to mention a recollection that the Sacrament of Orders is given but once!), and a single act of consecration conveys all the lines at once.

For instance, when I was ordained a bishop, the letter accompanying the certificate of ordination from my consecrator specifically stated that he had conveyed the succession from his primary consecrators (+Mathers and +Starkey); with the implication that only these lines were validly conveyed during the sacrament. Though he himself had exchanged lines a number of times over the years, these exchanges were not included. (However he did freely provide information on these exchanges of consecrations.)

But are lineages able to be "passed along" in some mystical way through the tactile succession? Do they pass in the laying on of hands, part of the beauty of the spiritual family tree? In the opinion and observation of a number of us ISM bishops, yes.

I propose that all episcopal lineages received by a bishop from all participating consecrators are necessarily passed on to any new bishops during ordination. Selective conveyance of lineages is not possible—and to insist on such is a misunderstanding of the grace of consecration.

As we will see in chapter 9, the situation becomes less clear on the issue of passing Inner Priesthood or Initiatic lines, where there may be unique initiatic requirements for the tradition. However, the theory and practice remain intact: the esoteric *succession* is conveyed according to the appropriate form, even if what is needed to "activate" it for the tradition has not yet been received.

RULE 5: BISHOPS EXCHANGING LINES CONVEY ALL THEIR LINES TO EACH OTHER

Now we're in the deep end of the pool. While Rules 1 through

4 must be considered any time an ISM bishop is ordained, this last Rule pertains to ISM bishops only if and when they perform non-sacramental consecrations with fellow bishops for the purpose of obtaining, bestowing, or sharing additional episcopal lineages.

Note here that it is bishops (those who have been validly ordained to the episcopate) who are exchanging lineages. A priest cannot begin to receive episcopal lineages prior to her/his becoming an ordained bishop.

The notion that consecrations received after one has been ordained a bishop must follow the rite of ordination of a bishop was present from the beginning of this practice in the early 20th century. It likely was an extension of the ecclesiology around conditional consecrations—bishops who wanted to exchange lineages simply adopted the most applicable rite.

This is exactly the right thinking—whether it was fully understood as such by our forebears or not.

As we've noted, while ordination provides an indelible mark on the soul, consecration is not so exclusive, and may be repeated with no disrespect to the Spirit or dilution of the rite. I know this is cutting a fine line, but I must argue for what I see is the work of the Spirit in cracking open a traditional practice precisely in order to introduce new insights and perspectives—and to recover long-forgotten wisdom.

A CASE STUDY

The example of one of the ISM pioneers found in many ISM bishops' episcopal family tree may help illustrate some of the rules in play.

Carmel Henry Carfora was initially ordained a bishop in 1912 by Paolo Miraglia Gulotti into the Vilatte succession from the Syrian Orthodox Church. Later, after he had become acquainted with the work of the Old Roman Catholic Church (the Mathew succession) in the Upper Midwest of the US, he came to have doubts about the validity of the Vilatte succession, and so was conditionally consecrated by HSH Rudolphe, Prince de Landas, Berghes in 1916. From here he lived and worked the rest of his life as an Old Roman Catholic bishop—and believed that this 2nd consecration was the sacrament. A number of his successors to this day hold the same opinion.

This is not, however, the last word. In Cafora's day, Vilatte's Orders were being widely disputed by the Episcopal Church and others to discredit him. Even Vilatte's ordainers seem to have been pressured to deny the validity of his ordination. In this light, Carfora's decision to receive a conditional ordination as bishop into the Old Catholic succession seem justified in order to vouchsafe his own work as a bishop and guarantee the validity of the sacraments done at his hands.

In recent years, some very welcome scholarship has confirmed that Vilatte was indeed properly and validly ordained a bishop for his American mission by prelates of the Syrian Orthodox Church. Carfora was mistaken in thinking he had not received a true ordination passed through Vilatte. While Carfora felt the Vilatte line of succession was not valid, we can now see that it indeed does conform to the criteria of validity from Alvares to Vilatte to Gulotti to Carfora. As such, Carfora was made a bishop by the Sacrament of Ordination in 1912 by Gulotti; his consecration by Landas, Berghes in 1916 did not have the weight of sacrament, but was instead a consecration into the Old Catholic line.

I present this situation here not to make our heads spin, but to illustrate that adjudicating validity in the ISM can sometimes be a moving target, even when everyone involved has the best intentions. This example also shows how, through Carfora, his successors in fact received both the sacramental Syrian Orthodox line from Vilatte and the additional Old Catholic episcopal lineage from Landas, Berghes. How one chooses to emphasize the influences of these two lineages in one's own episcopacy is a matter of the leading of the Holy Spirit.

NAGGING DOUBTS

The ISM community as a whole has inherited our founding bishops' anxiety about the validity of our orders in the face of condemnation by our mainline counterparts. We come by this honestly, passed down through generations of our forebears. We have come to believe that the bogeyman rightfully lives among us. And the relentless criticism from our mainline colleagues only fuels the ongoing issue. But our concerns are misplaced, and our mainline colleagues are in error in presuming they have authority to question our orders.

To my fellow ISM bishops, I can only say: *there is simply no possibility of ISM bishops ever doing enough to be considered true colleagues and peers by all our mainline confreres.* For the Orthodox—even those churches who conveyed their apostolic succession to Western bishops with the commission to go forth and replant Orthodoxy in Western Europe—there is no grace or episcopacy outside their jurisdictions. For Catholics and Anglicans, we are at best considered "valid, but irregular," and typically dismissed as fringe folks.

This is *especially* true once we succumb to the belief that by getting more lineages, we're somehow getting closer to being truly valid. And this has continued to be the primary source of mockery against us over the decades.

My question to my ISM colleagues is: why do we care? Validity is an "on/off" switch. One is either a valid apostolic bishop, or not. As we've seen in Rule 1, only within a communion can validity of sacraments be determined; and in Rule 2, that the ordaining bishops bear direct responsibility to assure validity. We need to stop the hand-wringing about validity. It dishonors the sacrament we have received and the Spirit Who has bestowed it.

Frankly, we need to be smarter and wiser about the theology of orders, and especially its particular manifestation in the ISM. We ISM bishops have, as a group, displayed an ignorance of the distinction between ability and authority to be bishops, and do much to discredit ourselves in the eyes of our mainline Anglican, Catholic, and Orthodox colleagues.

By unquestioningly accepting the misplaced condemnation by our mainline brethren, we have granted them the right to judge us.

I am, in fact, *not* arguing that we should not share our lineages with each other. Some (including myself) have, in fact, quipped that we should round up all the ISM bishops, lock ourselves in a stadium somewhere, and do one final grand exchange of lines so that all are equal, all share all lines, and we can just exhale and get on with ministry!

I hope by now it is plain in this book that I am proposing we play on our own field, recognizing the Spirit is doing something different with the ISM. If we are going to squander our energies on doubt, let it be the concern that we are doing enough in our commitment to minister to those who have been given into our pastoral and episcopal care.

PROPOSAL FOR AN AUTHENTIC WAY FORWARD

The churches and clergy of the Independent Sacramental Movement journey along two paths. The first is our common inheritance as sacramental communities: we are heirs to the full body of sacramental Christian practice and teaching reaching back 2000 years, and transmitted faithfully through the proper ordaining of bishops. We walk this path as do all sacramental jurisdictions—and we find our nuanced expression of practice and teaching as do each of our fellow sacramental jurisdictions.

We also travel a unique path that is still emerging and taking shape in the ISM. The majority of jurisdictions and denominations through history came to define themselves as *divergences* from a parent organization, typically over an interpretation of doctrine or practice. The ISM, on the other hand, often exhibits a fascinating *convergence* of practice and teaching: an ability and willingness to listen to the many strands of Tradition, and to apply wisdom to a new day, whatever its source among our faith ancestors. Episcopal Lineage prompts this sort of adventure, as we understand the many strands of Tradition passing into and through our ISM bishops.

I have faith that the Holy Spirit *is* inviting the ISM communions along this emerging path. Because of this, I believe that we ISM bishops must bring our "A game" if we are ever to lead those given into our care to become what the Spirit is asking us to become: dynamic and humble witnesses to the Good News, who minister in the margins and the way-places that our mainline denominational colleagues cannot or will not venture into. We are given different portions of the Harvest to attend to.

Throughout this book, I have tried to demonstrate that we as ISM faithful and especially as ISM bishops must change the game, and must own the conversation about our authenticity as faithful Christians. Inherent in our baptisms, confirmations, and ordinations as Independent sacramental Christians, the Holy Spirit invites and challenges us to own the following three declarations:

We Are Responsible for the Integrity of our sacraments. We must stop the bizarre notion among too many of us that an ISM bishop is an ordaining and consecrating machine who must run about making new clergy and bishops in order to prove her/his worth. Seriously, we need to take a collective breath, and find other ways to socialize as bishops!

That said, we must also embrace the insight that the Holy Spirit is using the ISM to call and send forth priests and bishops and baptized Christians in missional and unconventional ways that don't always resemble the organizational conventions of the last 1500 years. To all those truly called and sent, we owe the utmost care concerning our sacramants of initiation.

First and foremost, we must claim the foundational understanding that when a sacramental bishop is ordained, it is the Holy Spirit who ordains, through the instruments of sacramental bishops. This is the Church's understanding since the beginning, and continues to be upheld throughout sacramental churches around the world. Rightly made sacramental bishops are the cornerstone of ensuring that all the rest of the Church's sacraments are rightly done—in other words, are valid.

We ourselves must break the cycle of ignorance of the theology of orders, and the rampant idolatry of orders (coveting others' lines of succession). We ourselves must cultivate and teach the essential reverence for the action of the Holy Spirit in raising up worthy men and women to the Office of Bishop by ordination.

As long as an ordination fulfills the Augustinian (or Cyprianic, for those following Orthodox paths among us) criteria *as expressed by a faith community*, it only takes a single event to make a real sacramental bishop. And it only ever belongs to the community and bishops doing the ordaining to determine that the ordination was done in a "valid" way. It belongs to the ordaining bishops and the community (if any) to determine a bishop's *ability* to be a bishop. There are no other legitimate voices at the table on this matter.

When we re-set the conversation in this way, bishops in the ISM are as "valid" as any Roman Catholic, Orthodox, or Anglican bishop in the world. And as I've acknowledged in this book, bishops in the ISM will probably never be considered as equal colleagues with bishops of those communions. We need to get over it and banish the bogeyman.

We Are Responsible for the Shape of our Bishops' Authority. On whose authority were we called forth to become bishops? For what community or purpose? For many of us who grew up in conventional denominational life, we flounder on these questions, since our communities and ministries often do not easily map into the denominational model.

Yet we *have* been called forth. Some of us are called forth by existing communities of faithful, to accept the role of service as shepherd and pastor. Some of us are called forth by newly-forming communities to accept the role of visionary leader to shape the community in its period of formation. Some of us are called more mysteriously to wander, or minister incognito—to be stealth priests within communities that do not know they seek pastoral care. And some of us are called even farther afield to paths that do not look much like conventional ministry at all.

We must be clear: as with every other Christian communion, it is first and foremost the Holy Spirit who, by calling us forth to ministry and ordaining us through the Sacrament of Orders, grants us also the authority to live out our calling as the Spirit leads us.

As with every other Christian communion, there is more. As we saw in Chapter 1, Church leaders early on recognized the need to superimpose a hopefully discerning orderliness, and reserved for themselves the power to grant authority to bishops to exercise their ministries within the bounds of regional synods. In this, the Church abandoned its origin as loose overlapping confederations of wandering Elders, bringing the Good News wherever the Spirit led them, sometimes creating communities, sometimes just moving on.

As Independent sacramental bishops, we are called to a unique re-appraisal of this history and this constricting of the proclamation of the Good News.

Our authority as bishops, given by the Holy Spirit, and vouchsafed by our communities and ISM colleagues, is to become effective and tireless elders of our local ministries and communities, and advocates for the poor, sick, homeless, outcast. By the grace of God we too are vicars of the Christ, in whatever shapes and forms the Holy Spirit lead us. We need to own this.

We Are Responsible for the Gift of Episcopal Lineages. When I was considering writing this book, I conferred with ISM Bishop John Plummer. John has been active in the ISM longer than I, and is one of the folks I most respect for his considered thoughts on the unique contributions of the ISM to the Christian journey.

The central thought banging around in my head was this: in the same way that the Holy Spirit is using the discovery of lost scriptures to challenge the Church to embrace and include greater diversity of discourse, experience, and insight (truly to get back to the ancient church), I think there's something going on here in the Independent Sacramental Movement that challenges us to re-open our vision to the vast treasure house of other Christic traditions, to be open to mutual enrichment, and to recognize that we're already "spiritual cousins"—with our own unique voices. This manifests as episcopal lineages.

John's reply brought it to a sharp focus: "That's a very interesting line of thought, and follows the theological method that I lean toward: We presume that the Holy Spirit is active in our communities. We are doing X. Even if we are messed up in the way we are doing X, the Spirit is still hiding in there somewhere, redeeming our craziness. So how do we understand what is going on?"

How do we understand the phenomenon of episcopal lineages and multiple consecrations in the ISM, and what are the key touch points? Having faith that the Holy Spirit is at work within this phenomenon, what can we discover about it?

The spiritual potency of a line of succession that reaches back many centuries is a palpable thing. We ISM bishops stand at the end of a long line of bishops who dedicated and gave their lives to ministry and to the passing on of the particular spiritual practices, beliefs, and wisdom of a tradition.

The Spirit has given the ISM a unique role in Christian life, as re-weavers of the many threads of traditions into a luxuriant and lively fabric of faith.

A key part of our charism as the ISM is to be about the work of this re-weaving: to rediscover the astonishing rich diversity of spiritual life practiced over the past two millennia and to find creative ways to engage our present dark world with the best of those practices across all the threads of tradition. We won't all choose the same combination of threads and practices. But that is precisely a part of this living laboratory of faith that the Spirit is bringing forth among us.

We can and must retell the stories of the many peoples of the Christian Way as part of keeping the wisdom of their faith journeys alive as spiritual food for our local ministries and communities today. And as inspiration for charting our own ways forward in these new times.

Ultimately what matters most are the Sacrament of Orders, and the understanding of our own authority. These are the hallmarks of those called forth to be elders among us. Lineages add a texture and richness and flavor and color to our spiritual lives, and a sense of the spiritual family tree of which we're a part. We are invited to embrace this.

ISM SUCCESSION AND LINEAGES ILLUSTRATED

In this final section, I present my own episcopal succession and lineages as a means to illustrate the breadth of lineages received into the care of the ISM. From my researches I believe I have received every available source of apostolic lineage that has been conveyed into the ISM world, and have discovered and documented a few lines not mentioned by other researchers; I have received many of the available inner priesthood lineage sources as well.

My own lineage details are typical of North American ISM bishops; British and Continental ISM bishops will trace different lineal descent from the same sources.

For the sake of brevity, I include just one or two lines of succession for each source lineage. A complete document of successions for these lineages conveyed into my episcopacy can be found online at: **pelagios.net/succession.pdf**. Any additions or corrections to this document (which seems to be a never-ending process as information continues to come to light!) are most welcome and will be incorporated in the online version of this record to share with everyone and keep scholarship of our common inheritance freely available. Communications may be sent to me at **ism@pelagios.net**.

7. APOSTOLIC LINEAGES OF INDEPENDENT BISHOPS

WITH ALL THE DISCUSSION ABOUT ENSURING and preserving validity, how did ISM bishops get their orders? This chapter will attempt to give a more detailed glimpse of how the many sacramental lines were conveyed into the ISM world. (Chapter 8 will tackle the necessary task of discussing those lines that are claimed by bishops but that have a shadow of doubt on them.)

The vast majority of ISM bishops have received their Sacrament of Orders through the lines of a very small number of pioneers:

Rene Vilatte and Jules Ferrette—each owed their episcopacies and succession to the belief of the Syrian Orthodox Patriarch that Orthodoxy must be replanted in the West.

Aftimios Ofiesh—commissioned through the Russian Patriarchate in the first attempt at creating a pan-ethnic Orthodox jurisdiction on American soil.

Arnold Harris Mathew—ordained a bishop and chartered to establish the Old Catholic faith in Great Britain.

Antoine Joseph Aneed—pioneered an ecumenical participation among sacramental jurisdictions.

George Cummings—founded the Reformed Episcopal Church as a result of the first schism in the Episcopal Church in the US.

These few apostolic sources are the trunks of vast and luxurious spiritual family trees of bishops who can trace back to them. But there are quite a few more points of entry of mainline sacramental orders into the ISM. I have been privileged to receive into my care the apostolic lines in this chapter through my ordination as a bishop, and through subsequent consecrations.

For convenience and consistency, I have grouped the lines as per our discussion in Chapter 1 (Western Apostolic; Byzantine Orthodox; Oriental Orthodox ("Monophysite"); "Nestorian"; "Uniate").

☙

THE ANCIENT BRITISH/CELTIC CHURCHES IN IRELAND AND WALES

By tradition, the Good News was planted on the soil of Brittania even before the Church was established in Rome. Whether by the travels of Joseph of Arimathea, or by Roman slaves, or by traveling missionaries, the Church in Britain was sufficiently developed to send bishops to the Council of Nicea in 325. With the rise of Celtic culture, and travels of Coptic monks to Ireland, a unique flavor of Christian practice flourished for centuries. Scholars have long noted the congruence of Celtic spirituality and liturgy with that of the Eastern patriarchates, particularly Alexandria and Jerusalem.

Roman-style Christianity was introduced by Augustine, who was sent by Pope Gregory to evangelize the Britons/Celts in 597, where he set up his seat at Canterbury. For centuries, the two flavors of Christianity existed uneasily side by side. Celtic Christianity was based on the monastery, and the people were served by some local clergy, and numbers of Peregrinati, wandering abbot-bishops or monk-priests, who were practicing a uniquely Celtic austerity called the Green Martyrdom (forsaking home and kin to travel abroad for the Gospel). Roman Christianity, by contrast, had adopted the Roman civil model of administration by dividing the land into districts (dioceses), overseen by governors (bishops).

The Celtic Churches in Ireland and Wales, unlike those in England and Scotland, retained their independence and distinctive styles of organization up to the end of the 11th century. When the Irish and Welsh Churches adapted to the Roman model of episcopacy after the Norman conquest they did so by means of consecration from the existing bishops (another distinction from England and Scotland, where the native episcopates were entirely supplanted by Bishops in the Roman line) so that the Celtic succession became the principal line of succession in Ireland by the end of the 12th century.

Irish line from the ancient Celtic church. The succession from the Ancient Celtic/British Church in Ireland passed into the Anglican succession of the Church of England at several points in time. Notable successions from the ancient Celtic line in Ireland (see Anglican line in this document):

Archbishop John Cumin of Dublin, in 1199 assisted Gilbert Glanville in the consecration of William of S. Mere L'Eglise. Archbishop Christopher Hampton of Armagh (the historic seat of St. Patrick), in 1616 assisted Archbishop George Abbot in the consecration of George Montaigne, the principal consecrator of Bl. William Laud. (Note: See updated Celtic lineage at www.pelagios.net/succession.pdf)

Welsh Line from Jerusalem. This line starts with James the Less who was the first bishop of Jerusalem (Acts 15). The See of Jerusalem as a patriarchal see was named as such in AD 451, at the Council of Chalcedon.

1. JAMES the Less: recognized by the other Apostles as the Bishop of Jerusalem; 2. Simeon; 3. Justus I; 4. Zaccheus; 5. Tobias; 6. Benjamin; 7. John I; 8. Matthias; 9. Philip; 10. Seneca; 11. Justus II; 12. Levi; 13. Ephraim; 14. Joseph; 15. Judas; 16. Marcus; 17. Cassianus; 18. Publius; 19. Maximus I; 20. Julian; 21. Caius; 22. Symmachus; 23. Caius II; 24. Julian II; 25. Maximus II; 26. Antonius; 27. Capito; 28. Valius; 29. Daleanus; 30. Narcissus; 31. Dius; 32. Germanio; 33. Gordius; 34. Alexander; 35. Nazabancs; 36. Hymenacus; 37. Zamboas; 38. Herman; 39. Marcarius I; 40. Maximus III; 41. Cyril; 42.

Herenius; 43. Hilary; 44. John II; 45. Praglius; 46. Juvenal; 47. Anastacius; 48. Martyrius; 49. Salutis; 50. Elias; 51. John III of Jerusalem; 52. ST. DAVID (Dewi of Wales): consecrated first Celtic Bishop of Mineva, St. David's, Wales (AD 519); 53. Cynog; 54. Teilo; 55. Ceven; 56. Morfall; 57. Haerwneu; 58. Elwaed; 59. Gwrnwen; 60. Llumverth; 61. Gwrgwyst; 62. Gwgan; 63. Eineon; 64. Clydawg; 65. Elfod; 66. Ethelman; 67. Elane; 68. Magelsgwyd; 69. Made; 70. Cadell; 71. Sadwrnfen; 72. Novis; 73. Sulhaithnay; 74. Idwall; 75. Asser; 76. Arthwael; 77. Samson; 78. Reubin; 79. Rhydderch; 80. Elwin; 81. Morbiw; 82. Llunwerth; 83. Hubert; 84. Enerius; 85. Ivor; 86. Morgeneu I; 87. Nathan; 88. Jenan; 89. Arwystl; 90. Morgeneu II; 91. Ervin; 92. Trahacarn; 93. Joseph; 94. Bleiddud; 95. Salien; 96. Abraham; 97. Rhyddmarch; 98. Wilfrid; 99. Bernard; 100. D. Fitzgerald; 101. P. deLeia; 102. G. Camb; 103. G. deHenelawe; 104. Jowerth; 105. Gross; 106. deCarew; 107. T. Hech; 108. D. Martin; 109. H. Gower; 110. J. Thorsby; 111. R. Brian; 112. F. Fastolfe; 113. H. Doughton; 114. J. Gilbert; 115. G. deMona; 116. Henry Chichele: Bishop of the Celtic Church in Wales, St. Davids in 1408, made Archbishop of Canterbury by Rome (1414); 117. J. Stalford; 118. J. Kemp; 119. T. Bourchier; 120. J. Morton; 121. H. Dean; 122. W. Wareham, in 1533 assisted at the consecration of Thomas Cranmer, first Archbishop of the separated Church of England.

ANGLICAN: EPISCOPAL CHURCH IN THE USA (WM. M. BROWN)

At the founding of the United States as sovereign nation separate from Great Britain, the bishops of the English Church in the former colonies fled back to England, and those lay members of the Church of England who remained in the United States found themselves without episcopal leadership. While there were strong candidates for an American episcopacy, at that time the liturgy of consecration of the Church of England contained a clause that called for swearing allegiance to the British monarch. This was unacceptable to American leaders.

The Church of England in the 18th century was confronted with two parallel changes in the political climate that encouraged a new air of inclusivity. First, as England expanded its empire across the globe, indigenous branches of the Church of England took root, creating a demand for indigenous bishops. These bishops would not be any more prepared than the Americans to swear loyalty to the English crown. Second, the American Church was developing outside the English political sphere, and had secured valid consecration (of Samuel Seabury) from the Scottish Episcopal Church—meaning the American Church was not beholden to the Church of England. Canterbury quickly saw the benefits of an American episcopacy in union with the Church of England.

The English church relented and removed the loyalty clause from the consecration liturgy. William White and Samuel Provoost were the first Americans consecrated by the Church of England for the episcopacy of the newly separate Protestant Episcopal Church in the United States of America (White as bishop of Pennsylvania, and Provoost, bishop of New York).

Line from White (Anglican: Apostolic Catholic Church in England) through Wm. Brown. William White, bishop of Pennsylvania (PECUSA), who in 1827 consecrated: Henry V. Onderdonk, who on 7 July 1836 consecrated: Samuel Allen McCoskry, who on 8 December 1875 consecrated: W. E. McLaren, who on 24 June 1898, assisted by George F. Seymour and Cortlandt Whitehead consecrated: 1. William Montgomery Brown as Bishop of Arkansas, who on 2 January 1927 (after his departure from the ECUSA) consecrated: 2. Wallace David de Ortega Maxey, Mar David I, Supreme Hierarch of the Catholicate of the Americas, Bishop of the Apostolic Episcopal Church, who on 21 July 1947 assisted by Frederick Littler Pyman and Mathew Nicholas Nelson consecrated *sub conditione*: 3. Lowell Paul Wadle, Archbishop of the American Catholic Church, who on 22 June 1957 consecrated: 4. Herman Adrian Spruit, Church of Antioch, Malabar Rite, who on 3 July 1981 exchanged consecrations with: 5. Joseph Vredenburgh, Mar Narsai, Patriarch of the Federation of St. Thomas Christians on 26 July 2001, assisted by Virginia Vredenburgh, Mart'a Virginia, and Joseph Eaton, Mar Tooma II consecrated: 6. Robert Angus Jones.

ANGLICAN: REFORMED EPISCOPAL CHURCH IN THE US (CUMMINS)

Almost exactly 100 years after the founding of the ECUSA, the Protestant Episcopal Church in the USA experienced its first schism. George Cummins, Assistant Bishop of Kentucky, led a revolt against the rising tide of the Oxford movement and the Anglo-Catholic vogue in both the English and American churches. Cummins founded the Reformed Episcopal Church in 1873, and consecrated Charles Cheney, passing the historic Anglican line into a new jurisdiction. Cummins had received in his consecration the lines from both Seabury and White. (The succession from Cummins made possible the creation of the Free Protestant Episcopal Church, in England, a source for many Orders in the Independent world.)

Line from White (Anglican: Apostolic Catholic Church in England) to Cummins. William White, bishop of Pennsylvania (ECUSA), who on 31 October 1832 consecrated: John Henry Hopkins, who on 15 November 1866 consecrated: 1. George D. Cummins, Assistant Bishop of Kentucky. (continues also to Anglican: Free Protestant Episcopal Church)

Line from Seabury (Anglican: Apostolic Catholic Church in England) to Cummins. Samuel Seabury as Bishop of Connecticut (ECUSA), who on 17 September 1792, assisted by Bishops White, Provoost, and Madison (themselves consecrated by John Moore, Archbishop of Canterbury) consecrated: Thomas John Claggett as Bishop of Maryland (the first all-American bishop), who on 7 May 1797 consecrated: Edward Bass as Bishop of Massachusetts, who on 18 October 1797 consecrated: Abraham Jarvis as Bishop of Connecticut, who on 29 May 1811 consecrated: A.V. Griswold as Bishop of the Eastern Diocese, who on 31 October 1832 consecrated: John Henry Hopkins as Bishop of Vermont, who on 15 November 1866 consecrated: 1. George D. Cummins, Assistant Bishop of Kentucky. (continues also to Anglican: Free Protestant Episcopal Church)

Line from Cummins. 1. George D. Cummins, Assistant Bishop of Kentucky. Cummins left the Protestant Episcopal Church, and founded the Reformed Episcopal Church in 1873. On 14

December 1873 he consecrated: 2. Charles E. Cheney for the Reformed Episcopal Church, who on the 12 November 1912 consecrated: 3. Manuel Ferrando, for the Church of Jesus (Puerto Rico), briefly a mission diocese of the Reformed Episcopal Church, who on 19 September 1920 consecrated: 4. Henry van Arsdale Parsell for the Anglican Universal Church, who on 29 November 1936 assisted Georg Plummer and William Albert Nichols in consecrating: 5. Stanislaus De Witow (Witowski), who on 3 October 1964 assisted Joachim Souris in consecrating: 6. Walter Myron Propheta for the American Orthodox Catholic Church (later as Patriarch Wolodymyr I), who on 18 November 1971 performed an Economia on: 7. John Marion Stanley, Free Protestant Episcopal Church, later Mar Yokhannan, Orthodox Church of the East, who on 12 October 1989 consecrated: 8. Floyd W. Newman, Messianic Church in America, who on 7 February 1998 consecrated: 9. Joseph Vredenburgh, Mar Narsai, Patriarch of the Federation of St. Thomas Christians on 26 July 2001, assisted by Virginia Vredenburgh, Mart'a Virginia, and Joseph Eaton, Mar Tooma II consecrated: 10. Robert Angus Jones.

ANGLICAN: FREE PROTESTANT EPISCOPAL CHURCH (CHECKEMIAN)

Shortly after the founding of the Reformed Episcopal Church in the US, a similar discontent began in England, rejecting the increasing Catholicizing movement in the Church of England. In response to this, several non-CofE bishops came together to found a specifically Protestant Anglican jurisdiction to protect and continue the Protestant genius of the Anglican tradition. They elected Leon Checkemian, a wandering Armenian *vartapet* as their first Primus (see Armenian line). This new movement was called the Free Protestant Episcopal Church. Through the generosity of Alfred Richardson, an REC bishop, Cummins' Anglican Orders were transmitted to the UK to give the new jurisdiction clear Anglican Orders. While the FPEC bishops soon split from Nicholson, the transmission had already been accomplished.

An excellent history (and perhaps the only complete overview of this particular lineage) of the FPEC, by Bp. Darrel Hockley of the Old Protestant Episcopal Church can be found at: *http://net-ministries.org/see/churches/ch18802*.

Line from Cummins (Anglican: Reformed Episcopal Church) through Boltwood. George D. Cummins, Assistant Bishop of Kentucky. Cummins left the Protestant Episcopal Church, and founded the Reformed Episcopal Church in 1873. On 14 December 1873 he consecrated: Charles E. Cheney for the Reformed Episcopal Church, who on the 24 February 1876 consecrated: William Rufus Nicholson, REC, who on 22 June 1879 consecrated: Alfred Spencer Richardson, who (bringing the REC to England) on 4 May 1890, assisted by Charles Isaac Stevens of the Ferrette succession consecrated *sub conditione*: 1. Leon Checkemian, Mar Leon, 3rd British Patriarch of the Ancient British Church and First Primus of the Free Protestant Episcopal Church (also Armenian Uniate Titular Bishop of Malatia), who on 2 November 1897 consecrated: 2. Andrew Charles Albert McLaglen, Mar Andries, 4th British Patriarch of the Ancient British Church and Titular Bishop of Claremont, FPEC (also Primate of the United Armenian Catholic Church) who on 4 June 1922 consecrated *sub conditione:* 3. Herbert James Monzani-Heard, Mar Jacobus II, 5th British Patriarch of the Ancient British Church and Archbishop of Selsey, and Primus of the Free Protestant Episcopal Church (also Primate of the United Armenian Catholic Church). Primus Heard passed the primacy for the Ancient British Church and the United Armenian Catholic Church to Hugh George de Willmott Newman, Mar Georgius on 29 January 1945. Mar Georgius became the 6th British Patriarch. The primacy of the Free Protestant Episcopal Church was passed to William Hall. Heard, on 18 May 1939 consecrated: 4. William Hall for the Free Protestant Episcopal Church, who on 6 April 1952 consecrated: 5. Charles Dennis Boltwood. Boltwood would be the last Primus the united Free Protestant Episcopal Church. Boltwood on 3 May 1959 consecrated: 6. John Marion Stanley, Free Protestant Episcopal Church, later Mar Yokhannan, Orthodox Church of the East, who on 12 October 1989 consecrated: 7. Floyd Warren Newman, Messianic Church of America, who on 7 February 1998 consecrated *sub conditione*: 8. Joseph

Vredenburgh, Mar Narsai, Patriarch of the Federation of St. Thomas Christians on 26 July 2001, assisted by Virginia Vredenburgh, Mart'a Virginia, and Joseph Eaton, Mar Tooma II consecrated: 9. Robert Angus Jones.

ANGLICAN: PHILIPPINE INDEPENDENT CHURCH (PAGTAKHAN)

The story of the struggle of the Filipino people for a free and self-determining apostolic Church is a continual speaking of truth to power, and a continual trust in the Spirit to bring faith to fruition. The following is the briefest outline.

The twin colonialism of Spanish-controlled government and Roman Catholicism ensured that Filipinos were second-class citizens in their own country and their own Church. While Filipinos were welcomed into the ranks of clergy, none were allowed to attain the episcopate. In fact, in response to a petition by Fr. Aglipay, the Papal Nuncio responded that Filipinos were not capable of episcopacy.

Fr. Aglipay was eventually elected bishop by a group of clergy who withdrew from Rome to found a native and independent Church. For the next 50 years, the Church of two million Filipinos would struggle successfully in virtual poverty and without apostolic bishops. Their petitions to the Old Catholics and the Apostolic Episcopal Church for Orders were denied.

Initially, the Episcopal Church in the US also denied the Philippine Church a conveyance of apostolic succession. Finally, in 1948, they recognized the error in their original denial. Bishop Norman Binsted, the Missionary Bishop for The Philippines for the Protestant Episcopal Church (ECUSA), assisted by Bishop Robert Franklin Wilner and Bishop Harry Sherbourne Kennedy (ECUSA), passed on the Anglican succession to the Philippine Independent Catholic Church.

Line from White (Anglican: Apostolic Catholic Church in England) through Binsted. William White, bishop of Pennsylvania (later PB I & IV, ECUSA), who in 1832 consecrated: Benjamin Bosworth Smith, bishop of Kentucky (later PB IX, ECUSA), who in 1875 consecrated: Thomas U. Dudley, bishop of

Kentucky, who in 1893 consecrated: John McKim, bishop of North Tokyo, who in 1928 consecrated: Norman Spencer Binsted, missionary bishop for the Philippines (ECUSA) who on 7 April 1948 consecrated: Isabelo de los Reyes, Jr. Bishop de los Reyes had been elected Obispo Maximo of the PICC (Iglesia Filipina Independiente) in 1946. Bishop de los Reyes, assisted by Manuel N. Aguilar and Alejandro Remollino (PICC) on 22 September 1957 consecrated: 1. Francisco de Jesus Pagtakhan, who on 15 June 1988 consecrated: 2. Nils Bertil Alexander Persson, Metr. Bp. of the Western Orthodox Church. On 21 October 2001 there was a mutual exchange of consecrations with Bertil Persson, Francis Spataro, Paget Mack, Joseph Grenier, Patrick Trujillo, Joseph Gouthro, George Stallings, Bruce Simpson, Willard Schultz and with: 3. Peter Paul Brennan, Prime Bishop of the Ecumenical Catholic Diocese of America, who on 11 July 2004 exchanged consecrations with Timothy Michael Cravens, Independent Catholic Christian Church, and Richard Orville Blalock, Christ Catholic Church International, and with: 4. John Paul Aloysius Plummer, Mission Episcopate of the Theophany, who on 5 May 2006 exchanged consecrations with James Bryant of the Holy Orthodox Catholic Church of America and with: 5. Robert Angus Jones.

Line from Lea (Anglican: Apostolic Catholic Church in England) through Binsted. Arthur Lea as Bishop of Kyushu, who, assisted by Rolleston S. Fyffe, Bishop of Rangoon, and John McKim, Bishop of North Tokyo, in 1912 consecrated: Henry St. George Tucker as Bishop of Kyoto (later Virginia, later PB XIX ECUSA), who, assisted by John McKim, Bishop of North Tokyo, and John G. Murray, Bishop of Maryland (later PB XVI), in 1928 consecrated: Norman Spencer Binsted, missionary bishop for the Philippines (ECUSA) who on 7 April 1948 consecrated: Isabelo de los Reyes, Jr. Bishop de los Reyes had been elected Obispo Maximo of the PICC (Iglesia Filipina Independiente) in 1946. Bishop de los Reyes, assisted by Manuel N Aguilar and Alejandro Remollino (PICC) on 22 September 1957 consecrated: 1. Francisco de Jesus Pagtakhan (see above).

ANGLICAN: THE METHODIST CHURCH (WESLEY)

John Wesley was a priest in the Church of England in the 1700s. As a leader of the evangelical revival in England, he traveled extensively, preaching and forming prayer societies within the Church of England. His work eventually gave rise to Methodist societies in the American colonies. After the American Revolution (which he vehemently opposed by the way—a royalist to the end), Wesley was faced with the dilemma of providing pastoral oversight to his now orphaned American societies.

Claiming the precedent of Alexandria, in which a synod of presbyters elected and consecrated a new bishop to continue the Alexandrian succession, Wesley claimed to himself the prerogative to make "superintendents" for the American Methodists. Unlike his Alexandrian forebears, Wesley acted alone, and consecrated Thomas Coke solo, using the Prayer Book rite for consecrating a bishop. Coke had no sooner crossed the Atlantic and consecrated Asbury solo then the two men began calling themselves "bishop," which enraged Wesley. In this series of actions, the Methodist Church was born as a separate denomination, first in the new United States and later in Britain.

There has been much discussion in the past two hundred years about whether Wesley had been secretly ordained a bishop. We must remember that it was at the time illegal for any bishops other than Church of England bishops to be made and to function in England. If indeed Wesley *had* received ordination by non-Anglican hands, he was at risk of imprisonment for the offense.

Bertil Persson adopts the common claim that Wesley was quietly ordained to the episcopacy by a Moravian bishop on their shared voyage to the Georgia colony in the 1730s. No Methodist, Moravian, or independent documentation has ever surfaced to support such a claim. A careful study of Wesley's biography and writings, and the activities and writings of his Moravian colleagues, yields no evidence that he was ever recognized or honored as such by the Moravians, his Methodist societies, or anyone else; nor did his brother Charles ever let on such an event had transpired—and Charles was not shy about putting his criticisms of John in writing. Wesley himself did not begin to act the part of bishop—apostolic or not—until the mid 1780s, some fifty years after the conjectured ordination.

If one needs to find an apostolic connection, it is most probably that it was by the Cyprian Orthodox bishop Erasmus, who was on the scene at that time and had ordained preachers for Wesley. For a compelling reasoning of this position by a Methodist scholar, see the 1878 article "Was Wesley Ordained a Bishop by Erasmus?", *The Methodist Quarterly Review* 1878, online at: *http://wesley.nnu.edu/wesleyantheology/mreview/1870/A%201878%20Was%20Wesley%20Ordained%20Bishop%20by%20Erasmus%2088-111.htm*

I believe the simplest explanation is the most likely: that Wesley became convinced of the reality of the "scriptural episcopacy" of priests in unique need, based on the Alexandrian precedent, to fulfill his mission.

Wesley's actual succession into the ISM is included here because of the interesting possibility he was consecrated by Erasmus, and the far greater possibility that he was an early E.V. pioneer who passed on Anglican Orders via the Alexandrian precedent; and because his lineage was recognized and welcomed by the founders of the Reformed Episcopal Church, who included it into their own, as follows:

Anglican: Apostolic Catholic Church in England. Bl. William Laud as Bishop of St. David's (1626 Bath, 1628 London, 1633 Canterbury), who in 1658 consecrated: Niles Sancroft, Bishop of Oxford, who in 1683 consecrated: Dr. Philip Tillotson, Bishop of Oxford, who in 1701 consecrated: Dr. Baxter Tenison, Bishop of Oxford. Bishop Tenison ordained John Wesley as priest of the Church of England in 1724. 1. Fr. John Wesley on 2 September 1784 consecrated solo: 2. Thomas Coke, first Superintendent of the American Methodist Societies, who, by authorization from Wesley, on 27 December 1784 sailed to America and consecrated: 3. Francis Asbury as second Superintendent of the American Methodist Societies. Coke and Asbury changed their title to "Bishop". Asbury, assisted by Methodist Bishop Richard Whatcoat, on 18 May 1808 consecrated: 4. William McKendree who, assisted by Bishops Robert Roberts and Enoch George, on 27 May 1824 consecrated: 5. Joshua Soule who, assisted by Bishops William Capers and John Emory, in May 1852 consecrated: 6. Matthew Simpson, who assisted Reformed Episcopal Church Bishops George David Cummins and Charles Edward Cheney on 24 February 1876 in consecrating: 7. Bishop William Rufus Nicholson (continue through Anglican: Reformed Episcopal Church).

OLD CATHOLIC: UNION OF UTRECHT (GUL)

The conversion of the Netherlands to Christianity was due chiefly to the labors of St. Willibrord in the late 7th and early 8th centuries. After his consecration by Pope Sergius in 696, he established a Chair at Utrecht, Holland. Utrecht became the Primatial See of Holland, and ultimately became a Prince-Bishopric of the Holy Roman Empire until 1528, when Prince-Bishop Henry of Bavaria ceded the sovereignty to the Emperor Charles V. The Archbishop of Utrecht had secured a number of unique rights for the Dutch Church, which allowed them to conduct ecclesiastical matters with a great deal of freedom from Rome. Over time, Rome looked for opportunities to reverse this situation.

In 1702, the Roman Catholic Church in Holland (comprising the Archiepiscopal See of Utrecht and the Bishoprics of Haarlem and Deventer) became separated from the rest of the Roman Church when Pope Clement XI suspended the Archbishop, Peter Codde, resulting from political intrigue. The Dutch Church had chosen to harbor Jansenist refugees from Rome, and dared to oppose the Jesuits.

After the death of Archbishop Codde, Dominique Marie Varlet, Roman Catholic Bishop of Babylon, restored the apostolic succession. The Dutch Church became the Old Roman Catholic Church, to distinguish it from those who adhered to a new hierarchy imposed on Holland by the Roman Church.

The Vatican Council of 1870 is a dividing line in the history of the Western church. Vatican I introduced the dogma of Papal Infallibility. From points all across Europe, faithful Roman Catholics now found themselves at odds with their Church, and a surprising number turned to the Old Roman Catholic Church for Holy Orders for their clergy, and priests for their parishes. Those Catholics who departed the Roman Church over this dogma became known as Old Catholics, and many of their churches came together with the Dutch Church in the Union of Utrecht.

In the following table, the succession is traced from Cardinal Antonio Barberini, nephew of Pope Urban VIII. Barberini was nominated to the Archiepiscopal See of Rheims by King Louis XIV of France, recognized by the Pope, and the record of whose entry and enthronement at Rheims is preserved in Fisquot's *La France Pontificale;* so:

Utrecht Succession to Gul. 1. Cardinal Barberini, on 12 November 1668, consecrated: 2. Duc Charles Maurice Le Tellier as his perpetual "Coadutor cum jure successionis," who on 21 September 1670 consecrated: 3. Jacques Benigne Bossuet, Bishop of Mequx, who in 1673 consecrated: 4. Jacques Goyon de Matignon, Bishop of Condom, who on 12 February 1719 consecrated: 5. Dominique Maries Varlet, Bishop of Babylon, who on 18 October 1739 consecrated: 6. Peter Johann Meindaarts, Archbishop of Utrecht, who on 11 July 1745 consecrated: 7. Johann Van Stiphour, Bishop of Haarlem, who in 7 February 1768 consecrated: 8. Gualtherus Michael van Niewenhuizen, who in 21 June 1778 consecrated: 9. Johannes Broekman who in 5 July 1797 consecrated: 10. Johannes Jacobus van Rhijn who in 7 November 1805 consecrated: 11. Gijsbertus Cornelius de Jong who in 24 April 1814 consecrated: 12. Willibrordus van Os who in 25 April 1819 consecrated: 13. Johannes Bon who in 13 November 1825 consecrated: 14. Johannes van Santem who in 17 July 1853 consecrated: 15. Hermanus Heijkamp who in 11 August 1873 consecrated: 16. Casparus Johannes Rinkel who in 11 May 1892 consecrated:

European Line from Gul. 1. Gerardus Gul, 17th Archbishop of Utrecht, who, assisted by Edward Herzog (Old Catholic Church in Switzerland) in 1916 consecrated: 2. Henricus Johannes Theodorus van Vlijmen, 13th Bishop of Haarlem, who, assisted by Edward Herzog and Georg Moot (Old Catholic Church in

Germany) in 1920 consecrated: 3. Franciscus Kennick, 18th Archbishop of Utrecht, who on 14 September 1924 consecrated: 4. Adolf Kury, 2nd Old Catholic Bishop of Berne (Switzerland) who, assisted by van Henricus Johannes Theodorus Vlijmen and Johannes Hermannus Berends (bishop of Deventer) on 8 May 1935 consecrated: 5. Erwin Kreuzer, 5th Old Catholic Bishop of Bonn (Germany) who in 1939 consecrated *sub conditione*: 6. Albert Dunstan Bell as bishop for the North American Old Roman Catholic Church, who on 9 March 1940 consecrated *sub conditione*: 7. Edgar Ramon Verostek as bishop for the North American Old Roman Catholic Church, who on 7 December 1941 exchanged consecrations with: 8. Lowell Paul Wadle, Archbishop of the American Catholic Church, who on 22 June 1957 consecrated: 9. Herman Adrian Spruit, Church of Antioch Malabar Rite, who on 3 July 1981 exchanged consecrations with: 10. Joseph Vredenburgh, Mar Narsai, Patriarch of the Federation of St. Thomas Christians on 26 July 2001, assisted by Virginia Vredenburgh, Mart'a Virginia, and Joseph Eaton, Mar Tooma II consecrated: 11. Robert Angus Jones.

OLD CATHOLIC CHURCH OF GREAT BRITAIN AND IRELAND (MATHEW)

An Old Catholic Church was established in Great Britain and Ireland in 1908 when the Earl of Landoff (Arnold Harris Mathew) was consecrated as its first Bishop. In 1910, Bishop Mathew created a breach with Utrecht by consecrating two bishops for his church without first consulting the Utrecht bishops. Mathew, for his part, felt compelled to withdraw from the Utrecht church over several doctrinal and disciplinary issues, which he felt moved the church too far in the direction of Modernism and Anglicanism. By 1911, Mathew had published a "Declaration of Autonomy and Independence" for his English Church. Later that same year, Mathew's Church was received into union with the Orthodox Patriarch of Antioch. Yet he continued to seek affiliations with the Anglicans and the Roman Catholics—being rebuffed by both.

Throughout these early years, the membership and clergy of the Old Catholic Church of Great Britain and Ireland were in the vast majority active Theosophists and members of Blavatsky's Theosophical Society. Mathew was apparently aware of this situation, but did nothing. However, several years later Mathew suddenly expelled all of his Theosophist clergy, which had the effect of gutting his jurisdiction. These exiled clergy reorganized and founded the Liberal Catholic Church (see separate section).

Mathew raised the Austrian Prince de Landas Berghes to the episcopate in 1913. When World War 1 broke out a year later, the Prince went into exile in the United States. Being related to most of the royal houses of Europe, the British government ensured he would not be imprisoned in England as an 'enemy alien'. Prince Bishop de Landas Berghes ended up at St. Dunstan's Abbey in Illinois, meeting Abbot Francis Brothers, and raising both Brothers and Carmel Carfora to the Episcopate to further the Old Roman Catholic Church of America.

Line through Carfora. 1. Gerardus Gul, 17th Archbishop of Utrecht, who on 28 April 1908 consecrated: 2. Arnold Harris Mathew, 4th Earl of Landoff, Regionary Old Catholic Bishop for Great Britain and Ireland, afterwards Archbishop of London, who on 29 June 1913 consecrated: 3. His Serene Highness, Rudolphe Francois Edouard de Gramant Hamilton de Brabant, Prince de Landas, Berghes, et de Rache et Duc de St. Winnock, Archbishop of the Old Roman Catholic Church, who on 4 October 1916 consecrated *sub conditione*: 4. Carmel Henry Carfora, Archbishop & Primate of the North American Old Roman Catholic Church, who on July 30, 1942 consecrated *sub conditione:* 5. Hubert Augustus Rogers, North American Old Roman Catholic Church, who on June 21, 1952 consecrated *sub conditione:* 6. Cyrus A. Starkey, who on August 26, 1963 assisted Howard E. Mather in the consecration of: 7. Joseph Vredenburgh, Mar Narsai, Patriarch of the Federation of St. Thomas Christians on 26 July 2001, assisted by Virginia Vredenburgh, Mart'a Virginia, and Joseph Eaton, Mar Tooma II consecrated: 8. Robert Angus Jones.

Line through Brothers. 1. Gerardus Gul, 17th Archbishop of Utrecht, who on 28 April 1908 consecrated: 2. Arnold Harris Mathew, 4th Earl of Landoff, Regionary Old Catholic Bishop for Great Britain and Ireland, afterwards Archbishop of London, who on 29 June 1913 consecrated: 3. His Serene Highness, Rudolphe Francois Edouard de Gramant Hamilton de Brabant, Prince de Landas, Berghes, et de Rache et Duc de St. Winnock, Archbishop of the Old Roman Catholic Church, who on 3 October 1916 consecrated: 4. William Henry Francis Brothers, who on 24 March 1927, assisted by Archbishop Josef Zielonka of the Polish Catholic Church of America, consecrated *sub conditione:* 5. Wallace David de Ortega Maxey, Mar David I, Supreme Hierarch of the Catholicate of the Americas, Bishop of the Apostolic Episcopal Church, who on 21 July 1947 assisted by Frederick Littler Pyman and Mathew Nicholas Nelson consecrated *sub conditione*: 6. Lowell Paul Wadle, Archbishop of the American Catholic Church, who on 22 June 1957 consecrated: 7. Herman Adrian Spruit, Church of Antioch, Malabar Rite, who on 3 July 1981 exchanged consecrations with: 8. Joseph Vredenburgh, Mar Narsai, Patriarch of the Federation of St. Thomas Christians on 26 July 2001, assisted by Virginia Vredenburgh, Mart'a Virginia, and Joseph Eaton, Mar Tooma II consecrated: 9. Robert Angus Jones.

OLD CATHOLIC: MARIAVITE CATHOLIC (KOWALSKI)

The Mariavite Catholic Church began as a Roman Catholic Third Order, found temporary shelter in the Old Catholic Church of Utrecht, and moved on into the Independent world chiefly through the increasingly original visions of its leader, Maria Franciska Kozlowska.

The Mariavite Catholic Church was first founded in 1883 when Fr. Kasimir Przjemski, a Roman Catholic priest, gathered a group of priests who followed the Third Order of St. Francis. In 1886, a devout Roman Catholic lay woman, Maria Franciska Kozlowska joined them. Maria began having visions of the Virgin Mary in 1893, through which she was guided to form a mixed order dedicated to Our Lady. She then established the Mariavite motherhouse near Warsaw. Maria became known as Sister Felicya.

Roman Catholic authorities got wind of Sister Felicya's visions, and excommunicated the whole community in 1906. The core of the Mariavite teachings was centered on Mary, rather than Jesus. Sister Felicya taught that salvation lay in patterning one's life on that of Mary. Correlative to her visionary theology, Sister Felicya preached a social agenda of feminism that supported self-sufficiency for women.

The Mariavites found support through Utrecht, and in 1909 Archbishop Gul, assisted by Bishop Mathew, consecrated Johann Kowalski as Archbishop of Felicianov and Primate of the Old Catholic Church of the Mariavites. This union was short-lived. By WWI, Bp. Kowalski was teaching the ordination and consecration of women, as well as a doctrine of mystical marriage, which may have been an institutionalized free love. Utrecht immediately broke all relations with the Mariavites.

The Mariavites have continued to the present as independent jurisdictions, surviving internal schisms over doctrine (one group returning to it's Catholic roots, and the other developing such teaching as that Sister Felicya was the mystical wife of Christ, and expanding the Trinity to a Quaternity).

1. Gerardus Gul, 17th Archbishop of Utrecht, assisted by Arnold Harris Mathew (Old Catholic Church of England), Johannes Jacobus van Thiel and Nicolas Batholomaeus Petrus Spit (Old Catholic Church of Holland) and Joseph Demmel (Old Catholic Church of Germany) who on 5 October 1909 consecrated: 2. Johann Michael Kowalski as Primate of the Mariavite Catholic Church, who on 4 September 1938 consecrated: 3. Paul Fatome (Marc Marie) as Regionary Bishop for France, who on 6 October 1949 consecrated: 4. Helmut Norbert Maas (Paulus) as Bishop of the Mariavite Catholic Church in Germany, who on 24 May 1953 consecrated: 5. Efrem Maria Mauro Fusi as Bishop for the Mariavite Catholic Church in Italy (Chiesa Cattolica Mariavita), who on 26 May 1954 consecrated: 6. Clement Alfio Sgroi Marchese as Bishop of Sicily for the Mariavite Catholic Church in Italy, who on 18 September 1954 consecrated: 7. Hugh George de Willmott Newman, Mar Georgius I, Patriarch of Glastonbury and Catholicos of the West. On 10 April 1963 he consecrated: 8. John Marion Stanley, Free Protestant Episcopal Church, later Mar Yokhannan, Orthodox Church of the East, who

on 12 October 1989 consecrated: 9. Floyd Warren Newman, Messianic Church of America, who on 7 February 1998 consecrated *sub conditione*: 10. Joseph Vredenburgh, Mar Narsai, Patriarch of the Federation of St. Thomas Christians on 26 July 2001, assisted by Virginia Vredenburgh, Mart'a Virginia, and Joseph Eaton, Mar Tooma II consecrated: 11. Robert Angus Jones.

OLD CATHOLIC: LIBERAL CATHOLIC (WEDGWOOD)

The Liberal Catholic Church came into existence in 1917-1918 as the result of a complete reorganization of Mathew's Old Catholic movement in Great Britain.

Beginning in 1908 with his own consecration as Old Catholic bishop for England and Ireland, Arnold Harris Mathew in turn consecrated three bishops for his fledgling Old Roman Catholic Church (see earlier section). His first congregations and clergy (and bishops) were almost entirely comprised of members of the Theosophical Society. But Mathew withdrew from the Old Catholic Church of Utrecht over what he considered tendencies towards Modernism and Anglicanism among the Dutch church. In 1915 Mathew reversed his original acceptance of the Theosophists, and ordered his clergy to withdraw from the Theosophist Society. When they refused, Mathew declared the Old Catholic Church terminated. The former clergy of Mathew's church regrouped as the Liberal Catholic Church. Bishop Willoughby, though not a Theosophist, passed on the episcopacy via the Mathew line by consecrating James Wedgwood.

Bishop Wedgwood was an energetic missionary for the new LCC. He consecrated Charles Leadbeater in Sydney, Australia. Wedgwood and Leadbeater translated the Tridentine Liturgy into English, and imbued this liturgy a more joyous approach to worship, excluding from it what they viewed as excessive fear of God and cries for mercy. The new liturgy was also imbued with core theosophical concepts, though not burdened with theosophical vocabulary.

During the tenure of Regionary Bishop Hampton, the LCC split into two factions, the "Liberal Catholic Church, Province of the

US" retaining the fullness of the Theosophical beliefs, and the "Liberal Catholic Church International" (LCCI) adhering to a more traditional non-esoteric Old Catholic belief system, and revising the liturgy to a more Tridentine form.

Line through Hampton. 1. Gerardus Gul, 17th Archbishop of Utrecht, who on 28 April 1908 consecrated: 2. Arnold Harris Mathew, 4th Earl of Landoff, Regionary Old Catholic Bishop for Great Britain and Ireland, afterwards Archbishop of London, who on 28 October 1914 consecrated: 3. Frederick Samuel Willoughby, LCC, who on 23 February 1916 consecrated: 4. James Ingall Wedgwood, as Primate, LCC, who on 13 July 1919, assisted by Charles Leadbeater consecrated: 5. Irving Steiger Cooper, as First Regionary Bishop, LCC, Province of the US, who on 13 September 1931 consecrated: 6. Charles Hampton, Second Regionary Bishop, LCC Province of the US. Bishop Hampton, thereafter, on 23 August 1945 exchanged consecrations with Wadle, Kleefisch, Maxey, and Aneed. 7. Wallace David de Ortega Maxey, Mar David I, Supreme Hierarch of the Catholicate of the Americas, Bishop of the Apostolic Episcopal Church, who on 21 July 1947 assisted by Frederick Littler Pyman and Mathew Nicholas Nelson consecrated *sub conditione*: 8. Lowell Paul Wadle, Archbishop of the American Catholic Church, who on 22 June 1957 consecrated: 9. Herman Adrian Spruit, Church of Antioch Malabar Rite, who on 3 July 1981 exchanged consecrations with: 10. Joseph Vredenburgh, Mar Narsai, Patriarch of the Federation of St. Thomas Christians on 26 July 2001, assisted by Virginia Vredenburgh, Mart'a Virginia, and Joseph Eaton, Mar Tooma II consecrated: 11. Robert Angus Jones.

Line through Leadbeater. 3. Frederick Samuel Willoughby, LCC, who on 23 February 1916 consecrated: 4. James Ingall Wedgwood, as Primate, LCC, who on 22 July 1916 consecrated: 5. Charles Webster Leadbeater, Regionary Bishop for Australia, LCC, who on 17 October 1926 consecrated: 6. Ray Marshall Wardall, Suffragan Bishop for the US, LCC, who on 14 September 1947 consecrated: 7. Edward Murray Matthews, LCC Province of the US, who on 2 October 1955 consecrated: 8. William Henry Daw, Liberal Catholic Church International, later of the

Independent Catholic Church International, who, on 10 August 1986, assisted by Thomas D. J. McCourt and Thomas Illtyd Thomas consecrated: 9. Donald William Mullan, Liberal Catholic Church of Ontario, later leading the LCCO into merger into Christ Catholic Church International, who on 21 November 1999, assisted by L. M. McFerran and Jerome Robben consecrated: 10. Richard O. Blalack, Diocese of the Good Shepherd, Christ Catholic Church International, who on 11 July 2004 exchanged consecrations with Timothy Michael Cravens, Independent Catholic Christian Church, Peter Paul Brennan, Prime Bishop of the Ecumenical Catholic Diocese of America, and with: 11. John Paul Aloysius Plummer, Mission Episcopate of the Theophany, who on 5 May 2006 exchanged consecrations with James Bryant of the Holy Orthodox Catholic Church of America and with: 12. Robert Angus Jones.

ROMAN CATHOLIC: MEXICAN NATIONAL CATHOLIC CHURCH

In the late 1920s, there was an assassination attempt on the lives of Mexican Presidente Plutarco Elias Calles and his cabinet members. The Presidente claimed to trace the culprits to the Roman Catholic prelates and clergy in Mexico. Because of this, he vowed to establish a Mexican National Catholic Church, independent of Rome.

Archbishop Carmel Henry Carfora, Primate of the North American Old Roman Catholic Church (whose Orders are Old Catholic), was invited to Mexico to pass on the episcopacy for this new Church. Three bishops were consecrated to initiate the Mexican hierarchy: Jose Joaquin Perez y Budar, Antonio Lopez Sierra, and Dr. Macario Lopez Valdes. The three were known as the Nationalistas.

Despite an auspicious beginning, the National Church failed to supplant the Roman Church. In 1972, the majority of the Mexican National Catholic Church formally converted to Orthodoxy and was received into the Orthodox Church in America, under a specially created Mexican Exarchy. Small remnants of the Church survived, notably in Los Angeles (+Fairfield) and Texas (+Parnell).

Gerardus Gul, 17th Archbishop of Utrecht, who on 28 April 1908 consecrated: Arnold Harris Mathew, 4th Earl of Landoff, Regionary Old Catholic Bishop for Great Britain and Ireland, afterwards Archbishop of London, who on 29 June 1913 consecrated: 1. His Serene Highness, Rudolphe Francois Edouard de Gramant Hamilton de Brabant, Prince de Landas, Berghes, et de Rache et Duc de St. Winnock, Archbishop of the Old Roman Catholic Church, who on 4 October 1916 consecrated *sub conditione*: 2. Carmel Henry Carfora, Archbishop & Primate of the North American Old Roman Catholic Church, who on 17 October 1926 consecrated: 3. Jose Macario Lopez y Valdes, Iglesia Ortodoxa Catolica Mexicana (Mexican National Catholic Church), who on 27 March 1930 consecrated: 4. Alberto Luis Rodriguez y Durand, Iglesia Ortodoxa Catolica Mexicana, who on 12 March 1955 consecrated: 5. Emile Federico Rodriguez y Fairfield for the Iglesia Ortodoxa Catolica Apostolica Mexicana, who on 2 June 1974 consecrated *sub conditione*: 6. Robert Norton, who assisted David Mark Johnson, American Orthodox Church (and also assisted by Mark I. Miller), on 28 September 1974 in consecrating: 7. Francis Jerome Joachim (Ladd) for the Western Orthodox Church in America, who on 10 May 1981 consecrated: 8. Alan S. Stanford, Mar Joseph Thaddeus I, for the American Orthodox Church, who on ? consecrated: 9. Michael Whitney, who on 4 February 1999 consecrated: 10. John Paul Aloysius Plummer for the Mission Episcopate of the Theophany, who on 16 June 2002 exchanged consecrations with: 11. Robert Angus Jones.

ROMAN CATHOLIC: BRAZIL (DUARTE COSTA)

Msgr. Duarte Costa rose to prominence in the 1930s as the Bishop of Botucatu, Brazil, where he was outspoken in his defense of the poor. He openly criticized both the Brazilian government and the Roman Catholic Church for their neglect and abuse of Brazil's disenfranchised populace.

For his defense of the defenseless, in 1937 +Duarte Costa was removed from office by Pope Pius XII, and named titular bishop of Maura (an "honorary" title with no actual jurisdiction).

+Duarte Costa openly criticized the Vatican government for its role in helping Nazi officials flee to South America at the close of World War II (criticisms which were viewed as absurd at the time, but have more recently been fully vindicated). He also openly criticized the Roman Catholic Church for its conservative positions on divorce and clerical celibacy, and declared papal infallibility a false dogma.

For his frank and courageous witness, Msgr. Duarte Costa was excommunicated by Pius XII on July 6, 1945.

On August 15, 1945 Msgr. Duarte Costa gave "Solene investidura da sacra episcopalis" to Salomeo Ferraz of the Ingreja Catolica Livre Brazil (Free Catholic Church of Brazil). This body appears to have been organized in 1936 and to have elected Ferraz Bishop.

Msgr. Carlos Duarte Costa's personal integrity is undoubted. He suffered considerable personal deprivation owing to the positions he adopted, which made him *persona non grata* with the Brazilian authorities.

The line of succession from +Duarte Costa came to the US in the following way:

Line through Corradi-Scarella. 1. Carlos Duarte Costa, who on 23 January 1949 assisted Luis Fernando Castillo-Mendez in consecrating: 2. Stephen Meyer Corradi-Scarella for the Western Orthodox Church in America, who, assisted by Duarte Costa, on 15 August 1954 consecrated: 3. Emile Federico Rodriguez y Fairfield for the Iglesia Orthodox Catolica Apostolica Mexican, who on 20 March 1977 consecrated *sub conditione*: 4. Paul G. W. Schultz, who on 1 August 1992 consecrated *sub conditione*: 5. Jorge Enrique Rodriguez-Villa, who on 8 September 1997 consecrated: 6. Lawrence Stephen Terry, who on 25 April 1998 consecrated: 7. John Paul Aloysius Plummer for the Mission Episcopate of the Theophany, who on 16 June 2002 exchanged consecrations with: 8. Robert Angus Jones.

Line through Castillo-Mendez. His Holiness, Pope Leo XIII on 8 December 1882 consecrated: Cardinal Rampola del Tindaro, who 26 October 1890 consecrated: Cardinal Arcoverde de Albuquerque-Cavalcanti, who on 4 June 1911 consecrated: Sebastao Cardinal Leme de Silveira Cintra (Roman Catholic

Bishop of Rio de Janeiro), who on 8 December 1924 consecrated: 1. Carlos Duarte Costa, who on 3 May 1948 consecrated: 2. Luis Fernando Castillo-Mendez for the Igreja Catolica Apostolica Brasileira, who on 30 January 1985 consecrated *sub conditione*: 3. Forest Ernest Barber, who on 15 June 1988 consecrated *sub conditione*: 4. Paul G. W. Schultz, who on 1 August 1992 consecrated *sub conditione*: 5. Jorge Enrique Rodriguez-Villa, who on 8 September 1997 consecrated: 6. Lawrence Stephen Terry, who on 25 April 1998 consecrated: 7. John Paul Aloysius Plummer for the Mission Episcopate of the Theophany, who on 16 June 2002 exchanged consecrations with: 8. Robert Angus Jones.

Line through Cunha. 1. Carlos Duarte Costa, who on 5 June 1960 consecrated: 2. Milton Cunha, who on 3 October 1968 consecrated *sub conditione*: 3. Giuseppe Santo Eusebio Pace for the American Orthodox Catholic Church, who on 22 August 1972 consecrated: 4. Michel (Michael) Staffiero, who in November 1976 consecrated *sub conditione*: 5. Charles Richard McCarthy, who on 25 September 1977 consecrated *sub conditione*: 6. Charles David Luther for the Western Orthodox Church in America, who on 9 August 1982 consecrated: 7. Francis Jerome Joachim (Ladd) for the Western Orthodox Church in America, who on 26 June 1983 consecrated: 8. Justo Rogue Gonzales-Trimino for the Catholic Apostolic Church in North America (Patriarchate of Brazil), who on 24 September 1983 consecrated: 9. Carey Leopold Presson, who assisted Francis Joseph Ryan (Ecumenical Orthodox Catholic Church-Autocephalous) (also assisted by Joseph Ofton), on 13 April 1985 in consecrating: 10. Denis Mary Michel Garrison, who on 4 June 4 1988 consecrated *sub conditione*: 11. Steven Mark (Seraphim Symeon) Holdridge for the Holy Eastern Orthodox Catholic and Apostolic Church in North America (THEOCACNA), who on 8 September 1997 consecrated: 12. Lawrence Stephen Terry, who on 25 April 1998 consecrated: 13. John Paul Aloysius Plummer for the Mission Episcopate of the Theophany, who on 16 June 2002 exchanged consecrations with: 14. Robert Angus Jones.

Line through Ferraz. 1. Carlos Duarte Costa, who on 15 August 1945 consecrated: 2. Salamao Ferraz. (In 1958, Ferraz returned to the Roman Catholic Church as a bishop in the Archdiocese of Rio de Janeiro by order of Pope Pius XII. Already married, he was allowed to remain with his wife. Pope John XXIII appointed him Auxiliary of Rio de Janeiro. Pope Paul VI appointed him to one of the commissions working on Vatican II.) On 29 June 1951 he consecrated: 3. Manoel Ceia Laranjeira, who on 19 November 1969 consecrated: 4. Viktor Ivan Busa, who on 10 August 1972 consecrated: 5. Frederick Charles King in a mutual exchange of consecrations, who on 18 May 1975 consecrated: 6. Paul G. W. Schultz, who on 1 August 1992 consecrated *sub conditione*: 7. Jorge Enrique Rodriguez-Villa, who on 8 September 1997 consecrated: 8. Lawrence Stephen Terry, who on 25 April 1998 consecrated: 9. John Paul Aloysius Plummer for the Friends Catholic Communion, who on 16 June 2002 exchanged consecrations with: 10. Robert Angus Jones.

ROMAN CATHOLIC: VIETNAM (NGO DINH THUC)

Note: This line begins in the Chaldean Church of Babylon (see "Uniate" churches section for more history), but moves administratively into the Roman Catholic Church proper prior to transitioning to the Independent world.

The story of Bishop Ngo Dinh Thuc bound up with the story, on the one hand, of the political turmoil of Vietnam through the mid-20th century; and on the other hand, with the Roman Catholic sedevacantist and Marian visionary movements. It is difficult to find an unbiased accounting of the bishop's activities and thought processes. Only the barest outline is possible here, to provide a foundation for understanding how Roman Catholic succession moved into the Independent world through this bishop.

The Ngo Dinh family (Vietnamese names place the surname first, the given name last) were among the leaders of pre-communist Vietnam. Ngo Dinh's three brothers (one of whom was president) were killed in the early 1960s by the Vietnamese Communist authorities in the aftermath of the overthrow of the French-backed regime. Thuc himself escaped the same fate only because he was then attending the Second Vatican Council. After the Council, Archbishop Ngo Dinh was not allowed to return to Vietnam to resume his episcopal duties. He lived in exile first in Rome, and later in Toulon, France.

Ngo Dinh was induced to visit and investigate the community at Palmar de Troya, Spain, where several children and an adult claimed regular ongoing visions of the Virgin. Moved by heir faith and an initial belief that the visionary events and ecstasies were genuine, Bishop Ngo Dinh determined to convey Holy Orders on their adult leaders, including Clemente Dominguez y Gomez, the leading adult visionary. Those who were not already priests, he ordained before they were consecrated.

Ngo Dinh performed these acts without the approval of the Pope (Paul VI), who excommunicated Archbishop Ngo Dinh for his actions. The Archbishop quickly severed all ties with the Palmar de Troya community—whether because of his rebuke by the Pope or because he came to believe the Palmarians were a sham, or simply came to believe the community had defined itself in opposition to the Roman Church is the subject of debate. The effect was reconciliation to Rome. But Gomez and his followers were free to continue their journey, and the Palmarian bishops made new priests, who conducted regular masses for the many Palmarian faithful.

At the death of Pope Paul VI in 1978, Bishop Gomez claimed to have been mystically crowned Pope while in jail, founding the Palmarian Catholic Church, which continues to this day.

The remaining life of Archbishop Ngo Dinh is the stuff of controversy through to his death in 1984.

Maran Mar Yusip Ummanu'il II Thoma, Bishop of Seert of the Chaldeans, afterward Patriarch of Babylon of the Chaldeans, in 1917 consecrated: Francis Daoud, Bishop of Amadiyah of the Chaldeans, on 22 December 1929, assisted by Georges Dallal, Archbishop of Mossoul of the Syrians, and Jacques Nessimian, Archbishop of Mardin of the Armenians, consecrated: Antonin Drapier, Titular (Roman Catholic) Archbishop of Neocaesarea in Pontus, who on 5 May 1938, assisted by Isidore Dumortier, Titular Bishop of Lipara, and Ngo Ngoc Can, Titular Bishop of

Zenobias, consecrated: 1. Ngo Dinh Thuc, Pierre Martin, later of the Holy Palmarian Church, who on 11 January 1976 consecrated: 2. Clemente Dominguez y Gómez, later Pope Gregory XVII of the Holy Palmarian Church, who on 1 September 1977, assisted by Manuel Alonso Corral and Camilo Estevez Puga, consecrated: 3. Ciaran Bernardo Broadbery, who on xx April 1978 consecrated: 4. Michael Patrick O'Connor Cox (Cox left the Holy Palmarian Church in the early 1980s, since 1977 has been a member of the Order Mater Dei, and, since April 2000, has been the Archbishop and head of the Order), who on 19 May 1998 consecrated: 5. Patrick Buckley, who on 14 February 1999 consecrated: 6. Peter Paul Brennan, Prime Bishop of the Ecumenical Catholic Diocese of America, who on 11 July 2004 exchanged consecrations with Timothy Michael Cravens, Independent Catholic Christian Church, and Richard Orville Blalock, Christ Catholic Church International, and with: 7. John Paul Aloysius Plummer, Mission Episcopate of the Theophany, who on 5 May 2006 exchanged consecrations with James Bryant, Holy Orthodox Catholic Church of America and with: 8. Robert Angus Jones.

ORTHODOX CHURCH OF ALBANIA (NOLI)

The story of the Orthodox Church of Albania in the 20th century is inextricably tied to the story of the politic independence and ethnic self-awareness of the Albanian people.

In 1914 Albania became politically independent, and the Orthodox faithful reasserted themselves. The Church unilaterally declared autocephaly (from the Ecumenical Patriarch) in September 1922. In 1924 three priests (Teofan "Fan" Noli (Albanian American), Hierotheos (Greek), and Chrysostomos (Greek) were consecrated as bishops for the newly restored Church (consecrators unknown), and the three formed a Synod, naming Hierotheos as Archbishop.

Fan Noli was a literary luminary as well as political leader of the Albanian people in the US and in Albania. He was originally ordained by Metropolitan Platon to serve Albanian parishes in Massachusetts, under the banner of the Albanian Orthodox

Mission in America. Emigrating to Albania, Noli served as the Albanian delegate to the League of Nations, became briefly the Primate of the Albanian Church, and served as briefly as Prime Minister of Albania.

Disputes with the secular political authorities and the sister Orthodox jurisdictions created a period of flux, which was finally settled in April 1937, and Kristofor Kissi, a member of the Albanian Synod, was consecrated and installed as Metropolitan Archbishop (presumably by the Ecumenical Patriarch). The Communist government further interrupted the Albanian Church from the 1940s through the 1990s.

Archbishop Kissi, along with Archbishop Hierotheos, installed Noli as Metropolitan Archbishop for the American branch of the Church. A group of Albanians also formed the American Church, the Independent Albanian Orthodox Church of St. Paul, under the leadership of Archbishop Kristofor Rado about 1958.

Yahn of Athos, and Kristofor Kissi, Metropolitan of Tirane and Duressi, Archbishop of All Albania, in 1923 consecrated: Teofan "Fan" Noli, Metropolitan Archbishop of the Albanian Orthodox in the US, assisted Christopher Contageorge, who on 24 February 1946 consecrated: 1. Kristopher Rado, Independent Albanian Orthodox Church, who on 14 January 1965 consecrated: 2. Robert William Zimmer, N.A.O.R.C.C., who on 14 January 1965 consecrated: 3. Mikhael Francis Augustine Itkin, who on 21 September 1980 exchanged consecrations with: 4. Joseph Vredenburgh, Mar Narsai, Patriarch of the Federation of St. Thomas Christians on 26 July 2001, assisted by Virginia Vredenburgh, Mart'a Virginia, and Joseph Eaton, Mar Tooma II consecrated: 5. Robert Angus Jones.

AMERICAN ORTHODOX CATHOLIC (OFIESH)

The story of the American Orthodox Catholic Church is the story of ethnic Orthodox jurisdictions attempting to adapt to the American religious scene. This line combines the apostolic lineages of Greek, Albanian, Ukrainian, Russian and Syrian jurisdictions. This is also the story of Russian Orthodoxy trying to make its way in the world in the absence of its Patriarch.

As we saw on pp. 55-56, the Syrian Orthodox priest Aftimios Ofiesh came to New York to establish an English-speaking mission for immigrant Orthodox faithful. For this work he was ordained a bishop by the Russian Orthodox Church. Political jockeying between the Syrian, Russian, and Episcopal Churches nearly derailed his mission. Striking out on his own, Bishop Ofiesh established the first non-ethnic Orthodox jurisdiction on American soil thus:

Makarij III, Michael Neveskij, Metropolitan of Moscow (last head of the Russian Church before the restoration of the title Patriarch), who on 13 December 1903 consecrated: Evdokim Basil Meshcherskij, Archbishop of Alaska and All North America, who on 17 May 1917, assisted by Archbishop of Albania Kristofor Kissi consecrated: 1. Aftimios Ofiesh, Archbishop of Brooklyn for the Holy Eastern Orthodox Catholic Apostolic Church in North America (Syrian Orthodox mission), who on 27 September 1932, assisted by Sophronios Bishara and Joseph A. Zuk consecrated *sub conditione:* 2. William Albert Nichols as Archbishop Ignatius of Washington, D.C., who on 20 November 1933 with Samuel Gregory Lines consecrated: 3. Howard Ellsworth Mather, who, on 26 August 1963, assisted by Cyrus Starkey, consecrated: 4. Joseph Vredenburgh, Mar Narsai, Patriarch of the Federation of St. Thomas Christians on 26 July 2001, assisted by Virginia Vredenburgh, Mart'a Virginia, and Joseph Eaton, Mar Tooma II consecrated: 5. Robert Angus Jones.

ORTHODOX CHURCH IN AMERICA

The Orthodox Church in America began as the Alaska diocese of the Russian Orthodox Church. [Lest we forget, the Russians "owned" the northwestern coast of the US down to the San Francisco Bay until it was taken from them in the 1800s, and had a large and active fur trade throughout the northwest of the North American continent until Canada and the US forced them out.] The diocese eventually expanded into an exarchy for North America. The Church became autocephalous in 1970, and formally became the Orthodox Church in America.

1. Theophilus Pashkovsky and Arseny Chagovtsev of the

Orthodox Church in America (Russian Orthodox), who, assisting Aftimios Ofiesh, Archbishop of Brooklyn for the Holy Eastern Orthodox Catholic Apostolic Church in North America (American Orthodox Church), on 11 September 1927 consecrated: 2. Rizkallah Abo-Hatab, for the American Orthodox Church, who, assisting Aftimios Ofiesh, Archbishop of Brooklyn for the Holy Eastern Orthodox Catholic Apostolic Church in North America, and Elias II (Metropolitan of Tyre and Sidon of the Syrian Orthodox Patriarchate of Antioch and all the East) on 26 May 1928 consecrated: 3. Sophronios Bishara, who along with Rizkallah Abo-Hatab, on 25 September 1932, assisted Aftimios Ofiesh in consecrating: 4. Joseph A. Zuk, who on 27 September 1932, assisted Aftimios Ofiesh (along with Sophronios Bishara) in consecrating *sub conditione*: 5. William Albert Nichols as Archbishop Ignatius of Washington, D.C., who on 16 December 1933 with Samuel Gregory Lines consecrated: 6. Howard Ellsworth Mather, Mar Timothy, Exarch of the Order of Antioch, who, on 26 August 1963, assisted by Cyrus Starkey, consecrated: 7. Joseph Vredenburgh, Mar Narsai, Patriarch of the Federation of St. Thomas Christians on 26 July 2001, assisted by Virginia Vredenburgh, Mart'a Virginia, and Joseph Eaton, Mar Tooma II consecrated: 8. Robert Angus Jones.

ORTHODOX CHURCH OF CYPRUS

The Orthodox Church of Cyprus is one of the oldest autocephalous Orthodox churches, by Tradition founded by St. Barnabus. Its autocephaly was first recognized by the Council of Ephesus (431) and reaffirmed by the Council of Trullo (692). In spite of occupation by the French (1191-1489), the Venetians (1489-1571), and the Ottomans (1571-1832), the Church of Cyprus has always remained independent. This independence has enabled it to play an important role in the political life of the island. The church was active in the war of independence against the Turks. During the period of British control (1878-1958) the Cypriot church was at the forefront of the movement seeking union with Greece. On attaining independence in 1960, Archbishop Makarios III was elected as head of the new republic.

The tradition of combining the offices of head of state and head of church continued until the death of Archbishop Makarios in 1977.

Makarios II, Archbishop of New Justiniana and All Cyprus, who on 13 June 1948 consecrated: Makarios III, (Mikhail Christodolou Mouskos), Archbishop of New Justiniana and All Cyprus, who on ? consecrated: 1. Theoklitos Kantaris as Bishop of Salamis, Cyprus, who on 31 July 1966 consecrated: 2. John Arthur Chiasson for the American Orthodox Catholic Church, who on 7 December 1969 consecrated *sub conditione*: 3. Francis Joseph Ryan (Ecumenical Orthodox Catholic Church-Autocephalous), assisted by Carey Leopold Presson and Joseph Ofton, who on 13 April 1985 consecrated: 4. Denis Mary Michel Garrison, who on 4 June 1988 consecrated *sub conditione*: 5. Steven Mark (Seraphim Symeon) Holdridge, who on 8 September 1997 consecrated: 6. Lawrence Stephen Terry for the Holy Eastern Orthodox Catholic and Apostolic Church of North America (THEOCACNA), who on 25 April 1998 consecrated: 7. John Paul Aloysius Plummer for the Mission Episcopate of the Theophany, who on 16 June 2002 exchanged consecrations with: 8. Robert Angus Jones.

GREEK ORTHODOX: OLD CALENDAR SYNOD

Joachim Souris began his episcopal career in the Independent Movement, having been consecrated by Joseph Klimovicz of the Ofiesh lineage. It is important to note that the succession conveyed by Klimovicz was recognized as canonical by various Orthodox jurisdictions. However, Souris eventually converted to, and was received into, an Old Calendar Greek Orthodox jurisdiction, where he continued to function as a valid bishop.

1. Konstantin Kuryllo (Ruthenian Orthodox Church under the Russian Orthodox Church) who on 14 October 1930 consecrated: 2. Joseph Klimovicz for the Orthodox Catholic Patriarchate of America, who, assisted by Peter Andreas Zhurawetsky, on 2 June 1951 consecrated: 3. Joachim Souris for the Autocephalous Greek Orthodox Church, who, assisted by Stanislaus de Witow (Theodotus) on 4 October 1985 consecrated: 4. Timotheos

Athanasiou, Exarch Metropolitan of Montreal and the United States, who on 3 January 1994, along with Timotheos Mavias, consecrated: 5. Michael Seraphim Melchizedek, Greek Orthodox Eparchy of Lincoln, Nebraska, who on 25 January 1997 consecrated: 6. Michael Whitney, who on 4 February 1999 consecrated *sub conditione*: 7. John Paul Aloysius Plummer for the Mission Episcopate of the Theophany, who on 16 June 2002 exchanged consecrations with: 8. Robert Angus Jones.

RUSSIAN ORTHODOX CHURCH (KLEEFISCH)

According to ancient tradition, the Apostle St. Andrew first preached the Gospel of Christ in Russia and planted a cross at Kiev. The first recorded conversion of the Russian people to Christ was in 867, when missionaries arrived from Constantinople. In 988, St. Vladimir, Grand Prince of Kiev ordered his people to become Christian.

In 1589 Hieremias II, Ecumenical Patriarch of Constantinople, with the other ancient Patriarchates, granted the Russian Church autocephaly and raised Iov, Metropolitan of Moscow to the Patriarchal dignity. This created the Patriarchate of Moscow and all the Russias. During Russia's Civil War, patriarchal power was able to increase in strength rapidly, until civil power was restored. In 1700 Tsar Peter the Great took advantage of the death of Patriarch Aidan to turn the tables on the Church. With the consent of the other Patriarchs, he refused to allow the election of a new Russian Patriarch. In 1721 Peter suppressed the Russian Patriarchate entirely. A new constitution made the Tsar the Head of the Russian Church.

In 1917, when Tsar Nikolai II was overthrown, the leadership of the Russian Church met to elect a new Patriarch: Metropolitan Tikhon. As Metropolitan, Tikhon had governed the Russian Church in America before being recalled to Russia. The Bolsheviks imprisoned Patriarch Tikhon in 1922. The Bolshevik government refused to allow an election for Tikhon's successor when he died in 1925. Metropolitan Petr became Tikhon's *Locum Tenens*, but was also imprisoned. Sergii, Metropolitan of Nizhni-Novgorod succeeded Petr as *Locum Tenens*. Sergii became

Patriarch of the Russian Church in 1943, after gaining permission from Josef Stalin to hold patriarchal elections once more.

During 1917, foreseeing the continuing suppression of the Russian Church by civil authorities, Patriarch Tikhon issued a statement urging the Russian faithful to act independently to preserve the Russian Church. A number of actions were taken to establish the Russian Church outside of Russia. It was this statement that guided Metropolitan Sergii to consecrate Henry Kleefisch for work in the US

Henry Joseph Kleefisch was born and raised in the United States, and was originally ordained a Roman Catholic priest. He was an expert in Slavonic and Balkan languages. Kleefisch returned to the US and resided in San Francisco.

Sergij Stragorodskij, Metropolitan of Nizhni-Novgorod, afterwards Sergij, Patriarch of Moscow and all Russia. In 1917 at Irkutsk, Russia, assisted by Raban Ortinski, under a "canon of necessity" he consecrated: 1. Henry Joseph Kleefisch, who, along with Lowell Paul Wadle, Antoine Joseph Aneed and Charles H. Hampton, on 28 July 1946 consecrated: 2. Odo Acheson Barry, Mar Columba, who on 17 July 1955 consecrated *sub conditione*: 3. Hugh George de Willmott Newman, Mar Georgius I, Patriarch of Glastonbury and Catholicos of the West. On 10 April 1963 he consecrated: 4. John Marion Stanley, Free Protestant Episcopal Church, later Mar Yokhannan, Orthodox Church of the East, who on 12 October 1989 consecrated: 5. Floyd Warren Newman, Messianic Church of America, who on 7 February 1998 consecrated *sub conditione*: 6. Joseph Vredenburgh, Mar Narsai, Patriarch of the Federation of St. Thomas Christians on 26 July 2001, assisted by Virginia Vredenburgh, Mart'a Virginia, and Joseph Eaton, Mar Tooma II consecrated: 7. Robert Angus Jones.

RUSSIAN ORTHODOX CHURCH IN AMERICA (WENDLAND)

Konstantin Wendland became Metropolitan of the Russian Orthodox Church in America on 3 August, 1963. His tenure was brief, as he was recalled to the Soviet Union on 10 July 1967. In 1966, at the direction of the Russian Patriarch, Metropolitan

Wendland consecrated Joseph Skureth, who was then assigned as Exarch of the Western Orthodox Catholic Church in America (Exarchate of the Patriarchates of Moscow and Antioch). Bishop Skureth, through this, was likewise affiliated with the Syrian-Antiochene Orthodox Church.

Alexij Simanskij, Patriarch of Moscow and all Russia, on 28 December 1958 consecrated: Konstantin Nikolaevich Wendland, Ioann, Russian Orthodox Patriarchal Exarch in America, who, assisted by Dosifej Ivanchenko, on 17 April 1966 consecrated: 1. Joseph John Skureth, Joseph, Exarch of the Western Orthodox Catholic Church in America, who on 28 February 1989 consecrated: 2. Nils Bertil Alexander Persson, Metr. Bp. of the Western Orthodox Church. On 21 October 2001 there was a mutual exchange of consecrations with Bertil Persson, Francis Spataro, Paget Mack, Joseph Grenier, Patrick Trujillo, Joseph Gouthro, George Stallings, Bruce Simpson, Willard Schultz and with: 3. Peter Paul Brennan, Prime Bishop of the Ecumenical Catholic Diocese of America, who on 11 July 2004 exchanged consecrations with Timothy Michael Cravens, Independent Catholic Christian Church, and Richard Orville Blalock, Christ Catholic Church International, and with: 4. John Paul Aloysius Plummer, Mission Episcopate of the Theophany, who on 5 May 2006 exchanged consecrations with James Bryant of the Holy Orthodox Catholic Church of America and with: 5. Robert Angus Jones.

AMERICAN EXARCHATE OF THE RUSSIAN ORTHODOX CHURCH (FEDTSCHENKOV)

Succession has passed from the Russian Orthodox Church by several routes. Bishop Fedtschenkov established the American Exarchate of the Russian Orthodox Church. This Exarchate promoted a more accommodating stance with the Soviet government than the Russian Living Church faction of Kedrovsky.

1. John Athanasievich Fedtschenkov, Exarch of the Russian Orthodox Church, who in 1949 assisted Arsenio Saltas and Christopher Contageorge in consecrating: 2. Konstantin Jaroshevich, who on 19 September 1958 consecrated: 3. Charles

Dennis Boltwood, who on 3 May 1959 consecrated: 4. John Marion Stanley, Free Protestant Episcopal Church, later Mar Yokhannan, Orthodox Church of the East, who on 12 October 1989 consecrated: 5. Floyd Warren Newman, Messianic Church of America, who on 7 February 1998 consecrated *sub conditione*: 6. Joseph Vredenburgh, Mar Narsai, Patriarch of the Federation of St. Thomas Christians on 26 July 2001, assisted by Virginia Vredenburgh, Mart'a Virginia, and Joseph Eaton, Mar Tooma II consecrated: 7. Robert Angus Jones.

RUSSIAN ORTHODOX: THE LIVING CHURCH (KLIMOVICZ)

Joseph Klimovicz was ordained a priest in the Russian Orthodox Church, and was sent to the United States to do mission work in the northeast in 1912. The Russian Revolution left Russian Orthodox both at home and abroad in a state of confusion—leadership was disrupted and several factions among the faithful emerged, disagreeing on if and how the Church ought to cooperate and support the new Soviet State. Klimovicz found the American expression of the Russian "Living Church", headed in the US by John Kedrovsky.

Konstantin Kuryllo (Ruthenian Orthodox Church under the Russian Orthodox Church) who on 14 October 1930 consecrated: 1. Joseph Klimovicz for the Orthodox Catholic Patriarchate of America, who, assisted by Peter Andreas Zhurawetsky, John Cyril Sherwood, and Joseph Zielonka, on 2 June 1951 consecrated: 2. Joachim Souris for the Autocephalous Greek Orthodox Church, who, assisted by Stanislaus de Witow (Theodotus) on 1 July 1961 consecrated: 3. Walter Myron Propheta for the American Orthodox Catholic Church (later as Patriarch Wolodymyr I), who on 12 October 1969, assisted by Gregory Foster Gilead and John Chiasson (both consecrated by Propheta) consecrated: 4. David Mark Baxter, Orthodox Church of America, who on 6 August 1978, assisted by Paul Gilbert Russell, Holy Orthodox Catholic Church consecrated: 5. Theodore Thomas Peters, Holy Orthodox Catholic Church, who on 25 February 2001, assisted by Paul Gilbert Russell consecrated: 6. James Bryant, Holy Orthodox

Catholic Church of America, who on 6 May 2006 consecrated in a mutual exchange of consecrations John Paul Aloysius Plummer and: 7. Robert Angus Jones.

RUSSIAN ORTHODOX: THE LIVING CHURCH (VVEDENSKY)

Alexander Vvedensky is commonly regarded as the head of the Living Church during its years of Renovationist activities in the early decades of the 20th century. Though an unbiased understanding of this jurisdiction and its leadership is difficult to distill, the Living Church seems to have provided a more pro-Communist voice over against the Patriarch and hierarchs of the Russian Church, who were actively and determinedly anti-communist. His reasons for the consecration of Bishop Raines for the Russian Orthodox Church Abroad are not publicly available.

Alexander Vvedensky, at the request of John Kedrovsky of the Russian Living Church, on ? consecrated: 1. Maitland Ambrose Raines (Raynes), Russian Orthodox Church Abroad, who on 8 May 1934 assisted William Albert Nichols in consecrating: 2. George Winslow Plummer, Holy Orthodox Church in America, who on 29 November 1936 consecrated: 3. Stanislaus De Witow (Witowski), who on 3 October 1964 assisted Joachim Souris in consecrating: 4. Walter Myron Propheta for the American Orthodox Catholic Church (later as Patriarch Wolodymyr I), who on 18 November 1971 performed an Economia on: 5. John Marion Stanley, Free Protestant Episcopal Church, later Mar Yokhannan, Orthodox Church of the East, who on 12 October 1989 consecrated: 6. Floyd W. Newman, Messianic Church in America, who on 7 February 1998 consecrated: 7. Joseph Vredenburgh, Mar Narsai, Patriarch of the Federation of St. Thomas Christians on 26 July 2001, assisted by Virginia Vredenburgh, Mart'a Virginia, and Joseph Eaton, Mar Tooma II consecrated: 8. Robert Angus Jones.

SLAVONIC ORTHODOX (PRAZSKY)

After WWI, when Czechoslovakia gained political independence, it also experienced a significant conversion of its populace from Roman Catholicism to Orthodoxy. In 1921 the Serbian Orthodox bishop of Belgrade consecrated a native Czech to the episcopate for this new jurisdiction. In 1923 the Patriarchate of Constantinople granted autonomy to the new and growing Czechoslovakian Church.

During WWII, the Nazis virtually annihilated the Czech Church, and most of the clergy were sent to German labor camps. At the end of the war, the Soviet Union annexed much of the entire region, further destroying the remnant Church.

The Czechoslovakian Orthodox Church went underground in 1946. By one telling, the leadership of the Czech Church placed themselves under the protection of the Russian Orthodox Patriarch Aleksii I. By another telling, the Russian Orthodox Church attempted to take over and absorb the Czech Church. Some of the Czech bishops fled to the US and formed the Slavonic Orthodox Church, to protect the autonomous lineage. Bishop Prazsky renamed the Church after Bishop Filotej's death in 1970.

Noteworthy is the ecumenical relations between the Slavonic Orthodox Church and the Ukrainian Autocephalous Church in the USA. Metropolitan Prazsky (after a conditional consecration by Metropolitan Hryhorij Ohijchuk) served as head of both jurisdictions, though at his death, the leadership diverged once more.

Filotej of Presov, Metropolitan Archbishop of the Slavonic Orthodox Church; Vladimir of Debricin, and Ianofan of Uzhorod, on 5 May 1968 consecrated: 1. William Andrej Prazsky for the Autocephalous Slavonic Orthodox Church (in Exile), who, assisted by Anthony Prazsky, on 12 October 1969 consecrated: 2. Andre Penachio, Italian American Orthodox Catholic Church of the Americas, who on 17 September 1983 consecrated: 3. Joseph Alphonsus Fradale, Reformed Orthodox Church, who in October 1983 consecrated in a mutual exchange of lines: 4. Peter Paul Brennan, Prime Bishop of the Ecumenical Catholic Diocese of America. On 21 October 2001 there was a mutual exchange of consecrations with Nils Bertil Alexander Persson, Francis Spataro, Paget Mack, Joseph Grenier, Patrick Trujillo, Joseph Gouthro, George Stallings, Bruce Simpson, and Willard Schultz. 5. Peter

Paul Brennan, Prime Bishop of the Ecumenical Catholic Diocese of America, on 11 July 2004 exchanged consecrations with Timothy Michael Cravens, Independent Catholic Christian Church, and Richard Orville Blalock, Christ Catholic Church International, and with: 6. John Paul Aloysius Plummer, Mission Episcopate of the Theophany, who on 5 May 2006 exchanged consecrations with James Bryant of the Holy Orthodox Catholic Church of America and with: 7. Robert Angus Jones.

SYRIAN ORTHODOX "JACOBITE" CHURCH OF ANTIOCH (FERRETTE)

The Gospel was first preached in Antioch in Syria by Jewish converts returning there from Jerusalem after the Day of Pentecost, and later by refugees who fled Jerusalem during the persecution at the time of the martyrdom of St. Stephen.

St. Barnabas brought St. Paul from Tarsus and they went to Antioch ("the disciples were called 'Christians' first at Antioch"—Acts 10:26), and then on to Rome. St. Barnabas consecrated as his successor in Antioch St. Evedius, who was in turn succeeded by St. Ignatius, called "Theophoros." The 125th Patriarch of Antioch, counting from St. Peter, was Ighnatiyus Ya'qub II (1847-1872), upon whose instructions the future Mar Ighnatiyus Butrus IV (Peter III) consecrated Jules Ferrette, as Bishop of Iona. Mar Julius was given the mission of establishing indigenous Orthodox communities in Western Europe, autonomous of Antioch.

Returning to England, Mar Julius received Rev. Richard Williams Morgan, an Anglican priest, into Orthodoxy. Fr. Morgan, a Welsh nationalist and renowned folklorist, took the name Mar Morien I (the Welsh for Pelagius), and set about re-establishing the Ancient British Church.

Mar Ighnatiyus Butrus IV al-Ma'usili, Metropolitan of Emesa (Homs), afterwards Patriarch of Antioch and of All the Domain of the Apostolic Throne, with approval of Moran Mar Ighnatiyus Ya'qub II, Patriarch of Antioch and of All the Domain of the Apostolic Throne, on 2 June 1866 consecrated: 1. Raimond (Jules) Ferrette, Mar Julius, Bishop of Iona for the Syrian Orthodox (Jacobite) Patriarchate, who in 6 March 1874 consecrated: 2. Richard Williams Morgan, Mar Morien I, 1st British Patriarch, Ancient British Church, who in 22 June 1879, assisted by Frederick George Lee, Thomas Wimberly Mossman, and John Seccombe, consecrated: 3. Charles Isaac Stevens, Mar Theophilos I, 2nd British Patriarch, Ancient British Church, who on 4 May 1890, assisted by A. S. Richardson of the Reformed Episcopal Church consecrated *sub conditione*: 4. Leon Checkemian, Mar Leon, 3rd British Patriarch of the Ancient British Church and First Primus of the Free Protestant Episcopal Church (also Armenian Uniate Titular Bishop of Malatia), who in 1897 consecrated: 5. James Martin, Mar Jacobus I, Archbishop of Caerleon-upon-Usk, FPEC, who on 25 July 1915 consecrated: 6. Benjamin Charles Harris, Bishop of Essex, FPEC, who on 17 November 1944 consecrated: 7. Charles Leslie Saul, Mar Leofric, Archbishop of Suthronia in the Eparchy of all the Britons of the Protestant Evangelical Church of England, who on 6 June 1946 exchanged consecrations with: 8. Wallace David de Ortega Maxey, Mar David I, Supreme Hierarch of the Catholicate of the Americas, Bishop of the Apostolic Episcopal Church, who on 21 July 1947 assisted by Frederick Littler Pyman and Mathew Nicholas Nelson consecrated *sub conditione*: 9. Lowell Paul Wadle, Archbishop of the American Catholic Church, who on 22 June 1957 consecrated: 10. Herman Adrian Spruit, Church of Antioch Malabar Rite, who on 3 July 1981 exchanged consecrations with: 11. Joseph Vredenburgh, Mar Narsai, Patriarch of the Federation of St. Thomas Christians on 26 July 2001, assisted by Virginia Vredenburgh, Mart'a Virginia, and Joseph Eaton, Mar Tooma II consecrated: 12. Robert Angus Jones.

MAR THOMA (MALABAR) CHURCHES OF INDIA (VILATTE)

Note: this lineage is the sacramental line from my primary consecrator back through his primary consecrators. It is through this lineage that I received the Sacrament of Ordination to the episcopacy.

Christianity was first preached in India by the Apostle Thomas, and the indigenous church is known as "The Christians of St. Thomas," or more simply as "the Thomas Christians." The

Portuguese encountered this Church while exploring the Malabar Coast of India in 1498. The Thomas Christians, though then in full communion with the (Nestorian) Assyrian Church of the East, greeted the Portuguese as representatives of the Church of Rome.

The Portuguese brought in Roman Catholic missionaries and began imposing Latin custom and ritual. This culminated in the Synod at Diamper in 1599, where the Indian Church severed its ties with the Catholicos of the Assyrian Church. So thoroughgoing was the latinization of the Thomas Christian church that in 1653 most of the Church rebelled against this Westernization, and broke with Rome in an effort to regain their identity and historic church. The Thomas Christians split into no less than 5 jurisdictions. One faction returned to its historic relationship with the Assyrian Church of the East (see listing for Assyrian Church of the East); another allied with the Syrian Orthodox Church; another became a Uniate jurisdiction.

In 1665, one of those groups of Thomas Christians who remained separated from Rome found themselves without a bishop. They placed themselves under the jurisdiction of the Syrian Orthodox Patriarch of Antioch. This loose union provided the Thomas Christians with their ecclesial hierarchy, and they became the Syrian Orthodox Church of Malabar.

In the late 1800s, Joseph Rene Vilatte was ordained to the priesthood by Bishop Herzog of the Utrecht succession. He began is work in Wisconsin to create ethnic Old Catholic parishes. He immediately ran afoul of the Episcopal Church, which blocked his work, and damaged his relationship with Utrecht. Fr. Vilatte realized he needed episcopal authority to fully continue his work, but the door to Utrecht was closed (this was also on the heels of Utrecht's challenging relationship with Arnold Harris Mathew). Eventually Vilatte found sympathy and support from Mar Ighnatiyus Ya'qub II, the Syrian Jacobite Patriarch of Antioch and All the East, and through the Thomas Christian Archbishop of Ceylon, attained the episcopate. (This is a greatly condensed version of Vilatte's lengthy and controversial journey to establish indigenous churches in Wisconsin.)

There are two recorded origins for the Vilatte line: one from Moran Mar Ignatius Ya'qub II; the other from Moran Mar Ighnatiyus Butrus IV (Peter III), his successor. Both lead to Mar Julius I, Archbishop Alvares, who consecrated Vilatte.

Line through lines: Moran Mar Ighnatiyus Ya'qub II, Patriarch of Antioch and of All the Domain of the Apostolic Throne, on 12 February 1865 consecrated: Joseph Pulikottil, Mar Dionysios V, Metran of the Malankara Syrian Church (India), who, assisted by Paulos Mar Athanasius, Bishop of Kettayam (later Catholicos-Metropolitan of the Malankara Jacobite Syrian Church) & Legate of Moran Mar Ighnatiyus Butrus IV in Malabar, on 29 July 1889 consecrated: 1. Antonio Francisco Xavier Alvares, Mar Julius I, Archbishop of Ceylon, Goa and India for the Malankara Jacobite Syrian Church, who at the direction of Moran Mar Ignatius Butrus IV, Patriarch of Antioch and of All the Domain of the Apostolic Throne, and assisted by Paulos Mar Athanasius, on 29 May 1892 consecrated: 2. Joseph Rene Vilatte, Mar Timotheos, Archbishop of North America & Exarch of the American Catholic Church, who on 19 December 1915 consecrated: 3. Frederick E. J. Lloyd, Bishop of Illinois, afterwards Primate of the American Catholic Church, who on 1 July 1923 consecrated: 4. Gregory Lines, for the American Catholic Church, who on 16 December 1933 consecrated: 5. Howard Ellsworth Mather, who on 26 August 1963 assisted by Cyrus Starkey consecrated: 6. Joseph Vredenburgh, Mar Narsai, Patriarch of the Federation of St. Thomas Christians on 26 July 2001, assisted by Virginia Vredenburgh, Mart'a Virginia, and Joseph Eaton, Mar Tooma II consecrated: 7. Robert Angus Jones.

Line through Carfora. 2. Joseph Rene Vilatte, Mar Timotheos, Archbishop of North America & Exarch of the American Catholic Church, who on 6 May 1900 consecrated: 3. Paolo Miraglia Gulotti, who on 14 June 1912 consecrated: 4. Carmel Henry Carfora, Archbishop & Primate of the North American Old Roman Catholic Church, who on 30 July 1942 consecrated *sub conditione:* 5. Hubert Augustus Rogers, North American Old Roman Catholic Church, who on 21 June 1952 consecrated *sub conditione:* 6. Cyrus A. Starkey, who on 26 August 1963 assisted

Howard E. Mather in the consecration of: 7. Joseph Vredenburgh, Mar Narsai, Patriarch of the Federation of St. Thomas Christians on 26 July 2001, assisted by Virginia Vredenburgh, Mart'a Virginia, and Joseph Eaton, Mar Tooma II consecrated: 8. Robert Angus Jones.

AFRICAN ORTHODOX CHURCH (MCGUIRE)

In the early decades of the 1900s, Black Americans began to organize and look for ways and means to greater self-determination, and the creation of organizations that allowed for full participation and leadership. Fr. George McGuire led a very successful career as an Episcopal priest, but the Church had very few opportunities for non-Whites to become bishops. Fr. McGuire, who moved in the same circles as Marcus Garvey, led a community of Black faithful and clergy to create a new Church. The group approached the American Catholic Church to receive valid Orders from +Vilatte. The African Orthodox Church was founded in 1921, as a fully independent, new and ethnic jurisdiction, to serve Black Americans in the United States and the West Indies. It is one of the more successful of the Independent Churches, continuing to the present with over 2000 members.

Moran Mar Ighnatiyus Ya'qub II, Patriarch of Antioch and of All the Domain of the Apostolic Throne, on 12 February 1865 consecrated: Joseph Pulikottil, Mar Dionysios V, Metran of the Malankara Syrian Church (India), who, assisted by Paulos Mar Athanasius, Bishop of Kettayam (later Catholicos-Metropolitan of the Malankara Jacobite Syrian Church) & Legate of Moran Mar Ighnatiyus Butrus IV in Malabar, on 29 July 1889 consecrated: 1. Antonio Francisco Xavier Alvares, Mar Julius I, Archbishop of Ceylon, Goa and India for the Malankara Jacobite Syrian Church, who at the direction of Moran Mar Ignatius Butrus IV, Patriarch of Antioch and of All the Domain of the Apostolic Throne, and assisted by Paulos Mar Athanasius, on 29 May 1892 consecrated: 2. Joseph Rene Vilatte, Mar Timotheos, Archbishop of North America & Exarch of the American Catholic Church, who on 28 September 1921 consecrated: 3. George Alexander McGuire, African Orthodox Church, who on 10 September 1924 consecrated: 4. Arthur Stanley Trotman, African Orthodox Church, who on 8 August 1925, along with George Alexander McGuire and William Ernest James Robertson consecrated: 5. Reginald Grant Barrow, African Orthodox Church of N.Y., who on 11 May 1944 consecrated: 6. Cyrus A. Starkey, who on 26 August 1963 assisted Howard E. Mather in the consecration of: 7. Joseph Vredenburgh, Mar Narsai, Patriarch of the Federation of St. Thomas Christians on 26 July 2001, assisted by Virginia Vredenburgh, Mart'a Virginia, and Joseph Eaton, Mar Tooma II consecrated: 8. Robert Angus Jones.

ASSYRIAN CHURCH OF THE EAST (SOARES)

There is ample evidence to show that East Syria, Assyria, Persia, and Mesopotamia were evangelized by St. Thomas the Apostle assisted by St. Adai (one of the Seventy). One of their disciples, St. Mari, proceeded to Mylapore, where he preached the Gospel, according to the apocryphal Acts of Thomas.

According to the Book VI of the apocryphal Apostolic History of Abdias, the Apostles St. Simon and St. Jude also went to Persia, where they consecrated Abdias as Bishop of Babylon. The Assyrian Church (whose formal name is the Holy Apostolic Catholic Assyrian Church of the East) from its earliest days was governed by the Metropolitan of Seleucia-Ctesiphon, the twin capitals of the Persian Empire. The Metropolitan was subject to the Patriarch of Antioch and the East, but due to the distances and the difficulties in sustaining communications, patriarchal jurisdiction was granted to the Metropolitan, who was designated "Catholicos of the East and Patriarch."

The Assyrian Church of the East (ACE) was centered in the political sphere of the Sassanid Empire, which rivaled the Byzantine Empire. Political tensions entwined with theological tensions—as the bishops of the two regions split over the definition of the nature of Christ. The Church of the East gravitated towards the Antiochene form of Christology as articulated by Theodore of Mopsuestia and Nestorius. Nestorian Christians flocked into Persia following the condemnation of Nestorian teaching at the Council of Ephesus in 431 (thus formally separating the Church of the East from the rest of Orthodoxy), and the expulsion of Nestorians from the Empire by Emperor Zeno in the 480s.

The Church of the East at one time became the largest body of Christians in the world, extending its influence and jurisdiction throughout the Middle East, India, China, Japan and the Philippines. The Church of the East during this time was virtually the only variety of Christianity known in that part of the world. The Church was dealt a crushing blow by the rise of the Mongols. By the 15th century, the remnants of the Assyrian Church lived as refugees in the mountains of Kurdistan (Iraq).

In the 1550s the Church, in an effort to recover some of its traditions and former strength, elected a new Catholicos—but two rival successors were chosen, splitting the Church into two factions. One faction sought and secured support from Rome (see the Table "Chaldean Catholic Church"). From this period down to the present there have often been multiple rival lines of leadership in the Assyrian Church.

The Indian branch of the Church of the East (the Thomas Christians) remained in communion with the Catholicos until the Synod of Diamper (1559), when the Portuguese missionaries forced the Thomas Christians to sever their connection with the Assyrian Church and submit to Rome. Despite this shift of allegiances, a faithful remnant persevered, until in 1862 the Assyrian jurisdiction in India was restored, in this manner:

Line through Herford. His Sacred Beatitude, Maran Mar Shim'un XX, Rubil, Catholicos-Patriarch of the Church of the East, on 17 December 1862 consecrated: Antony Thondanatta, Mar Antonios Abd-Ishu, Metropolitan of India, Ceylon, Mylapore, Socotra and Messina, who on 24 July 1899 consecrated: 1. Luis Mariano Soares, Mar Basileus, Metropolitan of India, Ceylon, Mylapore, Socotra and Messina, who on 30 November 1902 consecrated: 2. Ulric Vernon Herford, Mar Jacobus, Bishop of Mercia and Middlesex, in whom in 1903 the above Metropolitan See also vested, on 28 February 1925 consecrated: 3. William Stanley McBean Knight, Mar Paulus, Bishop of Kent, who on 18 October 1931 consecrated: 4. Hedley Coward Bartlett,

Mar Hedley, Bishop of Siluria, who on 20 May 1945 consecrated *sub conditione:* 5. Hugh George de Willmott Newman, Mar Georgius I, Patriarch of Glastonbury and Catholicos of the West. On 6 June 1946 he exchanged consecrations with: 6. Wallace David de Ortega Maxey, Mar David I, Supreme Hierarch of the Catholicate of the Americas, Bishop of the Apostolic Episcopal Church, who on 21 July 1947 assisted by Frederick Littler Pyman and Mathew Nicholas Nelson consecrated *sub conditione*: 7. Lowell Paul Wadle, Archbishop of the American Catholic Church, who on 22 June 1957 consecrated: 8. Herman Adrian Spruit, Church of Antioch Malabar Rite, who on 3 July 1981 exchanged consecrations with: 9. Joseph Vredenburgh, Mar Narsai, Patriarch of the Federation of St. Thomas Christians on 26 July 2001, assisted by Virginia Vredenburgh, Mart'a Virginia, and Joseph Eaton, Mar Tooma II consecrated: 10. Robert Angus Jones.

Line through Heard. 1. Luis Mariano Soares, Mar Basileus, Metropolitan of India, Ceylon, Mylapore, Socotra and Messina, Ancient Church of the East, who in November 1932 consecrated *sub conditione:* 2. Herbert James Monzani-Heard, Mar Jacobus II, 5th British Patriarch of the Ancient British Church and Archbishop of Selsey, and Primus of the Free Protestant Episcopal Church (also Primate of the United Armenian Catholic Church). Primus Heard passed the primacy for the Ancient British Church and the United Armenian Catholic Church to Hugh George de Willmott Newman, Mar Georgius on 29 January 1945. Mar Georgius became the 6th British Patriarch. The primacy of the Free Protestant Episcopal Church was passed to William Hall. Heard, on June 13, 1943 consecrated: 3. William Bernard Crow, Mar Basilius Abdullah III, Patriarch of Antioch of the Ancient Orthodox Catholic Rite; who on 10 April 1944 consecrated: 4. Hugh George de Willmott Newman, Mar Georgius I, Patriarch of Glastonbury and Catholicos of the West. On 6 June 1946 he exchanged consecrations with: 5. Wallace David de Ortega Maxey, Mar David I, Supreme Hierarch of the Catholicate of the Americas, Bishop of the Apostolic Episcopal Church, who on 21 July 1947 assisted by Frederick Littler Pyman and Mathew

Nicholas Nelson consecrated *sub conditione*: 6. Lowell Paul Wadle, Archbishop of the American Catholic Church, who on 22 June 1957 consecrated: 7. Herman Adrian Spruit, Church of Antioch Malabar Rite, who on 3 July 1981 exchanged consecrations with: 8. Joseph Vredenburgh, Mar Narsai, Patriarch of the Federation of St. Thomas Christians on 26 July 2001, assisted by Virginia Vredenburgh, Mart'a Virginia, and Joseph Eaton, Mar Tooma II consecrated: 9. Robert Angus Jones.

GREEK MELKITE CATHOLIC CHURCH OF ANTIOCH (ANEED)

The word "Melkite" is derived from the Syriac and Arabic word "Melek" meaning "King," and literally means "royalist". Melkites were those members of the Greek Orthodox churches in ancient times who supported the decisions of the Council of Chalcedon (451) concerning the nature of Christ. The Council had the full support of the Byzantine Emperor, and those faithful who took refuge under his protection were labeled as loyalists (melkites). The Melkites remained within the Orthodox world, and in the Great Schism of 1054, remained allied in the East.

During the Middle Ages, a number of Melkite patriarchs made formal allegiances to Rome. Over time, two clear factions arose within the Church: one preferring autonomy with on-going contact with Rome; the other preferring autocephaly and relations with the Ecumenical Patriarch.

The Greek Melkite Catholic Church of Antioch began its life as a distinct Church in the 18th century, when a schism finally divided the pro-Orthodox and pro-Catholic factions of the Antiochene Patriarchate. Two rival patriarchs arose: Silbestros, who was recognized by the Patriarch of Constantinople and the Ottoman government as Patriarch of Antioch; and Kirillus VI, who was recognized by Pope Benedict XIII in 1729, and led his people in the new Uniate (an Eastern Church in full union with Rome) Church.

In 1848 the Ottoman government formally recognized the Melkite Church. In the present century, quite a number of Melkite faithful fled from Turkish persecution and from troubles of the two World Wars to the United States. In 1911 those who had already migrated to the US were visited by Bishop Aneed.

Kyrillus VIII Jiha, Melkite-Greek Patriarch of Antioch and All the East, of Alexandria and of Jerusalem, on 5 February 1905 consecrated: 1. Athanasius (Melece) Sawoya, Greek Melkite Metropolitan Archbishop of Beyrouth and Gebeil in Syria (former Roman Catholic Patriarch of Antioch), who on 9 October 1911 consecrated: 2. Antoine Joseph Aneed, Exarch of the Greek Melkite Rite in the United States, afterward Patriarch of the Byzantine Universal (Catholic) and Orthodox Church of the Americas. Aneed's consecration was recognized by Kirillus IX Mughabghab, Patriarch of the Melkite Catholic Church (1925-1947). Bishop Aneed on 24 November 1964 consecrated: 3. Emile Federico Rodriguez y Fairfield for the Iglesia Ortodoxa Catolica Apostolica Mexicana, who on 20 March 1977 consecrated *sub conditione*: 4. Paul G. W. Schultz, who on 1 August 1992 consecrated *sub conditione*: 5. Jorge Enrique Rodriguez-Villa, who on 8 September 1997 consecrated: 6. Lawrence Stephen Terry, who on 25 April 1998 consecrated: 7. John Paul Aloysius Plummer for the Mission Episcopate of the Theophany, who on 16 June 2002 exchanged consecrations with: 8. Robert Angus Jones.

CHALDEAN CHURCH OF BABYLON (LEFBERNE)

This is the Catholic counterpart of the Assyrian Church of the East, which broke with the Universal Church in 431 after the Council of Ephesus over the teaching of the nature of Christ (the Nestorian controversy).

From the 13th century, Roman missionaries were active in the Assyrian Church, but despite some individual conversions, no permanent union was formed. Then, in 1552, as a result of the election of the new Catholicos, rival factions chose two different leaders. Yuhannan Sulaka, one of the candidates, appealed to Rome for recognition, and in April 1553 Pope Julius III invested him as Patriarch of the Chaldean Church. In 1662 his successor Mar Shimun XIII repudiated this union with Rome. Mar Shimun XIII's successors have been the Patriarchs of the Church down to the present.

A group of the faithful who remained in communion with Rome were for many years governed by a line of Patriarchs all bearing the name Joseph. In July 1830 Pope Pius VIII suppressed the Josephite line, and declared John VIII Hormez to be Patriarch of Babylon of the Chaldeans, and as such, head of the Chaldean Catholic Church; of which:

Maran Mar Yusip Ummanu'il II Thoma, Bishop of Seert of the Chaldeans, afterward Patriarch of Babylon of the Chaldeans, in 1917 consecrated: 1. Antoine Lefberne, Mar Antoine, Patriarchal Exarch of Western Europe & Special Commissary in the United States, who on 4 May 1925 consecrated: 2. Arthur Wofert Brooks, Mar John Emmanuel, Titular Bishop of Sardis, afterwards Titular Archbishop of Ebbsfleet and Administrator of the Metropolitan Synod of the Apostolic Episcopal Church in the USA, who on 13 July 1946 consecrated *sub conditione:* 3. Wallace David de Ortega Maxey, Mar David I, Supreme Hierarch of the Catholicate of the Americas, Bishop of the Apostolic Episcopal Church, who on 21 July 1947 assisted by Frederick Littler Pyman and Mathew Nicholas Nelson consecrated *sub conditione*: 4. Lowell Paul Wadle, Archbishop of the American Catholic Church, who on 22 June 1957 consecrated: 5. Herman Adrian Spruit, Church of Antioch Malabar Rite, who on 3 July 1981 exchanged consecrations with: 6. Joseph Vredenburgh, Mar Narsai, Patriarch of the Federation of St. Thomas Christians on 26 July 2001, assisted by Virginia Vredenburgh, Mart'a Virginia, and Joseph Eaton, Mar Tooma II consecrated: 7. Robert Angus Jones.

8. WHEN IS A LINEAGE NOT A LINEAGE?

DUE TO THE FLUID AND DE-CENTRALIZED nature of the ISM, record-keeping has been at times difficult to obtain or verify, and some records have been lost at the death of a bishop. Compounding this, honest Western faithful have not always understood the nuances of Orthodox and Oriental Orthodox clergy ranks and titles.

From a purely human view, wishful thinking (to put as charitable a name on it as possible) about the availability of a lineage, and political machinations around lineages, have further complicated the whole matter.

All of this is a way of introducing the lineages in this chapter as problematic. Some lines simply lack documentation or first-person witness. Some lines are fictitious but claimed through honest misunderstanding. Some lines may be valid, but the truth is lost to us through deliberate actions by participants and/or detractors. And some lines are deliberate fabrications. I will try to pinpoint the issues, and discuss why a line is listed in this chapter.

One probably insurmountable problem with replacing bad information with good is the endless replication of errors in lineage records as bishops pass on their records to new bishops and share bad information without sufficient research. It is my hope that this chapter in particular will invite bishops to review and reflect on their own lineage records, and correct any errors.

I welcome any further documented information or well-reasoned discussion on these lineages, and will post new information and new questions on my web site at pelagios.net/ismpage.html. I invite my episcopal and scholarly colleagues to engage the same level of scrutiny on other lines of succession where the errors or doubt have been unknown to me.

Note: You will not find any lists of lineage succession in this chapter. I do not wish to perpetuate any of the errors that have permeated ISM bishops' own lineage documents. I have, however, preserved the claimed lines of succession traced from these sources in the complete research version of my lineages on my web site, solely for the purposes of research and discussion.

☙

ROMAN CATHOLIC LINE FROM +SANCHEZ Y CAMACHO

In the latter half of the 19th century, Msgr. Eduardo Sanchez y Camacho was a diocesan bishop in the Roman Catholic Church in Mexico. He had a falling out with his fellow bishops when he voiced support for the Mexican Revolution, and publicly opposed the promotion of the devotional of Our Lady of Guadeloupe. Ultimately, the Vatican sent Archbishop Averardi to mediate this dispute. The effort failed.

The Pope removed Msgr. Sanchez y Camacho from his see in October 1896. Sanchez left the Roman Catholic Church altogether, and became involved in efforts to found a Mexican National Catholic Church. These efforts would not bear fruit till the next century, when +Carfora was invited to Mexico to provide Holy Orders to the founders of a sanctioned National Church.

In 1899, while on a trip to Italy, Msgr. Sanchez y Camacho reportedly secretly consecrated Rev. Edward Donkin (an American Protestant minister) to further this effort at a national church. Donkin, in turn consecrated two British clergy: +Ulric

Vernon Herford, and +Herbert Monzani-Heard.

There has always been some dispute whether Rev. Donkin ever actually received episcopal orders from Bishop Sanchez y Camacho, but no decisive evidence or circumstance has ever been produced either way. Donkin's story, on the face of it, contains several problems: as a Protestant, Bp. Sanchez y Camacho should have first conditionally baptized, confirmed, and ordained Donkin to the deaconate and priesthood before ordaining him as a Catholic bishop. No mention has ever surfaced that this occurred. Further, a consecration in secret violates the Augustinian formula for valid consecration.

Contemporaries believed Donkin a fraud, and even the humble +Herford did his best to keep his conditional consecration by Donkin a secret.

Verdict: Because of this, I believe this lineage is not authentic, and should not be claimed by bishops as either a sacramental succession or an episcopal lineage.

ORDER OF CORPORATE REUNION

During the late 1800s, Anglican clergy were particularly concerned about the validity of their orders and succession. According to contemporary published accounts: at the direction of the Roman Catholic Church hierarchy at Venice in 1877, a highly secret plan was initiated for the purpose of introducing accepted (valid) Orders into a Pro-Roman Catholic Uniate movement within the Church of England. Roman Catholic Bishops, a Greek Bishop, and, purportedly, a Coptic Bishop, their names being kept secret under the Seal of the Confessional, but their validity guaranteed by the Roman Catholic Church in Rome, gathered for a secret ceremony. They are said to have conditionally re-baptized, re-confirmed, ordained as deacon and priest, and then ordained to the episcopacy two Church of England priests (Frederick George Lee, Thomas Wimberly Mossman) and a doctor (John Thomas Seccombe) as Catholic bishops.

From this origin point, the OCR line passes to Arnold Harris Mathew, Leon Checkemian, and William Albert Nichols, and down to their successors.

There is strong conflicting contemporary opinion concerning the veracity of claims of the original OCR bishops (see "A Statement of The Society of the Holy Cross Concerning The Order of Corporate Reunion" published in 1879, and available on the Project Canterbury site at *www.anglicanhistory.org/ssc/ocr.html*). By the admission of those consecrated, the consecrations for the OCR took place in great secrecy, which of itself invalidates the Sacrament of Orders according to Augustinian teaching.

No certificates of consecration or other documentation have ever been produced, and various lists of possible consecrators have been published through the years. However, even the Anglican critic Brandreth grudgingly concedes that the three original OCR bishops' claims were quite possibly true despite the lack of evidence. Several competing groups demonstrate lineal descent from one or more of the three purported original bishops.

Verdict: This lineage is problematic if we are to adhere to the Augustinian rules of the Sacrament of Orders, and even the rules of lineage. It is impossible to claim with anything like certainty a line through any tradition, since the names of the consecrators cannot be verified. I remain on the fence and have chosen to no longer report this as a line in my episcopacy. I recommend my colleagues also approach this line of succession thoughtfully and make their own determinations.

GREEK ORTHODOX PATRIARCHATE OF JERUSALEM

The history of the Greek Patriarchate of Jerusalem is the history of wars and conquering armies. Tradition from the earliest days of the Church records that James, the brother of Jesus, was the first bishop of the Christians at Jerusalem.

While the Church at Jerusalem is the Mother of all Churches, it was not until the Ecumenical Council of Chalcedon in 451 AD that the bishop of Jerusalem was granted Patriarchal dignity. The authority of the Patriarch was eclipsed when the Arabs conquered Jerusalem in 637. In 1099, Latin Christians conquered the Holy Land, and set up their own Latin Patriarch, though they were unable to unseat the Orthodox Patriarch. The Westerners were driven out by the Mamluk dynasty, who hated everything Christian. The centuries of shifting political ownership of Jerusalem ended in the 1800s, and the relative truce allowed the Greek Patriarchate to re-establish itself, now in a situation of multi-ethnic Orthodox populations.

A consecration into this line for Symeon Holdridge is reported to have occurred in 1983. Documentation for this consecration is reportedly no longer extant, and nothing is known of two of the three consecrators, either "Patriarch Markos of Alexandria (exiliar patriarchate)," or "Umile Natalino." Despite Bishop Holdridge's objections to my previously published doubt of this lineage (as reported to me by other bishops), multiple written requests by me directly to Bishop Holdridge for information—and the opportunity to correct my opinion—have not been acknowledged. Archbishop Bertil Persson is of the opinion that Patriarch Diodorus would not likely have participated in such a consecration, particularly only as a co-consecrator. Bishop Holdridge later joined the Holy Eastern Orthodox Catholic and Apostolic Church in North America (THEOCACNA) and was conditionally consecrated in 1988.

Verdict: Given the lack of attestation or documentation, and the absence of firm facts about the consecrators, I cannot vouch for the validity of this line of succession, and recommend that in the absence of evidence that bishops not claim succession or lineage from this source. I would welcome clarification from Bishop Holdridge on this fascinating event, and will happily publish his response and information on my website as noted at the top of this chapter.

COPTIC ORTHODOX/ ETHIOPIAN ORTHODOX LINES...

The Coptic Orthodox Church, by tradition, was founded by the Evangelist Mark, who was martyred in Alexandria in 63 AD. Alexandria was a pre-eminent theological center, and the Coptic Church was the birthplace of Christian desert monasticism. Alexandria opposed the vocabulary of the Christological formulae of the Ecumenical Council of Chalcedon. The opposition was at least as much based on politics as theology, as Alexandria viewed the Chalcedonian formula as being a Constantinopolitan error. Coptic Christianity became labeled Monophysite from this time, and the Alexandrian Patriarchate was viewed as having parted from the One Church. From this point, there were two Patriarchs: the Greek one (the Greek Orthodox Patriarchate of Alexandria), living in Alexandria, and the Coptic one (the Coptic Orthodox Church), living from the 5th to 9th centuries at the desert monastery of St. Macarius before returning to Alexandria. Both are titled "Pope," and their jurisdictions overlap.

The Ethiopian Orthodox Church was, by tradition, founded by St. Frumentius, a shipwrecked Christian from Tyre. Frumentius evangelized the country and was consecrated a bishop by St. Athanasius of Alexandria in the mid-4th century. In the next 100 years, key evangelizers in Ethiopia were those Eastern Christians fleeing the Chalcedonian jurisdictions. The Ethiopian Church derived her bishops, liturgy, and theology from the Coptic Pope, and all bishops of the Ethiopian Church have been Egyptian Copts. At many points over the intervening 1500 years, there was only one bishop for the whole of the Ethiopian Church, and he was an Egyptian Coptic bishop.

In the early 20th century the Ethiopian people pressed the Coptic Pope for a native episcopate, and autonomy in their affairs. In 1929 four native Ethiopian bishops were consecrated to assist the Coptic Metropolitan. Emperor Haile Selassie facilitated an agreement with the Copts, which allowed the election of an Ethiopian Metropolitan at the death of the then current Coptic Metropolitan. Thus in 1951, the assembly of clergy and laity of the Ethiopian Church elected Basilios, and the Ethiopian Church gained autonomy. In 1959 the Coptic Patriarch Kirillus VI Azir Yusuf 'Ata (Pope and Patriarch of the Great City of Alexandria and of All the Land of Egypt, of Jerusalem the Holy City, of Nubia, Abyssinia, and Pentapolis and All the Preaching of Mark) confirmed Metropolitan Basilios as the first Patriarch of the Ethiopian Orthodox Church.

I have yet to discover any bishop outside the canonical Ethiopian or Coptic jurisdictions who can claim actual lineage from these jurisdictions—and would welcome any documentation to the contrary.

...THROUGH +GABRE MICHAEL KRISTOS

In his lineage document, +Bertil Persson records that LaVon Miguel Haithman, a.k.a. Gabre Mikael Kristos, was made a Comos (archimandrite) by Abuna Basilios. The office of Archimandrite is akin to archpriest, but distinctly *not* a bishop. Therefore, Kristos did not have the Ethiopian/Coptic line to convey. However, as Kristos was made a bishop by James Hubert Rogers in 1971, he was acting in a valid episcopal way when he consecrated Philip Lewis in 1982. He just did not impart the Coptic line, since he never had it to convey.

Verdict: There is no Coptic/Ethiopian Orthodox line of succession here, and it should not be claimed by bishops as either apostolic succession or episcopal lineage.

...THROUGH +JOHN HICKERSON

The following is the line most often referenced by bishops claiming to possess Coptic lineage. John Hickerson (also reported as Hickersayon) began his ministerial career working as an evangelist with Father Divine. After some trouble with the police, Hickerson later emerged with an apostolic consecration from Edwin M. Jack of the Vilatte succession. Bp. Hickerson incorporated a church called the Coptic Orthodox Church Apostolic, in New York.

There is no credible evidence that Bp. Hickerson ever received Orders from a Coptic source. Even though +Davison Quartey Arthur, who was consecrated by Hickerson, went on to present "authentic-looking Coptic-style consecration papers" to Hugh George de Willmott Newman (who took them at face value and untranslated, and accepted Arthur as having a Coptic line), this seems to have been the only contemporary "research" into the veracity of the claim. And as it appeared to give de Willmott Newman an otherwise unobtainable ancient line of succession, it seems that there was no real effort to authenticate the claim. No actual line connecting Arthur or Hickersayon to the ancient

Ethiopian or Coptic Orthodox Churches has been discovered.

Perhaps of most interest, when the British Orthodox Church, de Willmott Newman's jurisdiction, sought and obtained full communion and integration with the Coptic Orthodox Church, the British Orthodox bishops based the validity of their Orders and Church on their succession through Ferrette and the Syrian Orthodox Church.

Verdict: It seems certain that this line is fictitious. I recommend bishops not claim this line as their apostolic succession or episcopal lineage.

...THROUGH +VAN ASSENDELFT-ATLAND

Jean Marie Blom van Assendelft-Atland was indeed received into the Coptic Orthodox Church after spending years as an ISM bishop. He was re-ordained by Pope Shenouda III. Some ISM bishops claim a consecration of C.C.J. Stanley by van Assendelft-Atland after his conversion. Ward doubts this occurred, and colleagues of Bishop Stanley state that Stanley himself denied that this consecration occurred. Further, Mark I. Miller does not acknowledge this line, and Alan Stanford notes its doubtful status (both of whom were consecrated by Stanley).

Verdict: It seems certain that this line is fictitious. I recommend bishops not claim this line as their apostolic succession or episcopal lineage.

ARMENIAN CATHOLIC CHURCH THROUGH +LEON CHECKEMIAN

The original foundation of the Holy Apostolic Church in Armenia may be traced to the Apostles: Saints Thaddeus and Eustatius, two of the Seventy, who suffered martyrdom about the middle of the 1st century. The honor of converting the Armenians, as a nation, to Christ was gained by St. Gregory the Illuminator, who in 302 was consecrated Archbishop of Etchmiadzine by St. Leontius, Exarch of Caesarea.

In the 12th century, some of the Armenians began to contemplate union with Rome, and the Catholicos was a guest of honor at the Latin Council of Antioch in 1141. During this period, the Armenians came into contact with the Crusaders, who were passing through Asia Minor en route to the Holy Land. The Armenians absorbed several Latin liturgical usages from the Crusaders. All of this culminated in a union between the Church of Rome and the Armenian Apostolic Church in 1198.

At the Council of Florence in 1439, a formal re-union of the two communions was proclaimed. Though no action was taken to make this a reality, it created the foundation for the emergence of the Armenian Catholic Church in later centuries.

Catholic missionary activity had begun among the Armenians in the 1300s. In 1742 Pope Benedict XIV raised an Armenian Apostolic Church bishop, Abraham Ardzivian (1679-1749) as Patriarch of Cilicia of the Armenias; he took the name Abraham Pierre I.

The Armenian Catholic Church faced the same interference under Ottoman rule, as did most other Churches in that empire and the Armenian people were terribly persecuted under the Turks.

According to *all* contemporary sources, including newspapers in England and in Armenia, writings by his English successors, and Checkemian's own written and verbal statements, Leon Checkemian was not in fact consecrated a bishop by Chorchorunian, or anyone else for the Armenian Catholic Church. He was, more accurately, lifted to the rank of *vartapet*: a unique rank in the Armenian Orthodox tradition. A vartapet assumes many of the administrative and pastoral duties of a bishop, but may not ordain to the major orders of clergy, and is not able (since he does not possess it) to pass along apostolic succession.

It appears that Checkemian initially attempted to play on the ignorance in the West of the office of vartapet, and claim for himself apostolic lineage from the Armenian Church. Yet even he recognized the limited value of this ruse, and arranged for consecration through the Ferrette lineage to demonstrate the validity of his position.

This information is also laid out on the British Orthodox Church's web site. The BOC is one of the most credible successors in the Checkemian line.

Verdict: There is no Armenian Catholic apostolic succession through Checkemian. I recommend bishops not record this as either their apostolic succession or episcopal lineage.

METHODIST LINEAGES

As a former Methodist, this one is a special pet peeve.

A number of bishops in the past few years have begun to claim a Methodist line of succession from +Cedarholm, who before he became an ISM bishop was a Methodist minister (and not a Methodist bishop). This is typically accompanied by some rather fanciful language about a "presbyteral succession" from Wesley, as well as a reference to Wesley's use of the Alexandrian solution (a number of priests may close a break in the episcopal succession by collectively electing and consecrating one of their own as a new bishop).

This claim is erroneous—for the purposes of the Sacrament of Orders and episcopal lineage—in two ways:

While the basis of most all Protestant practice is an ordination of a presbyter by other presbyters (or non-sacramental superintendents/bishops), there is no sacramental component to this ordinance. It simply does not equate to the whole understanding of sacramental Orders, which requires a valid bishop to ordain a presbyter/priest, and a sacramental intention and liturgical structure.

Any reference to the Alexandrian presbyteral solution interpreted as a continuing chain of succession from priest to priest cannot hold: the Alexandrian solution was a single unique event understood to repair the gap in succession. The ordaining priests never ordained another priest or bishop after this event.

This presbyteral succession claim must be kept distinct from the consideration of whether Wesley ever himself received an episcopal ordination from one of several speculated sources, or whether he chose to (imperfectly) emulate the Alexandrian solution to create valid (in Methodist terms) clergy for the Methodist Societies in the American territories.

The irony is that there is a demonstrable claim for lineage from Wesley through Methodist bishops down into the Reformed Episcopal Church, as demonstrated in the previous chapter. And Cedarholm possessed this documented lineage.

Verdict: The claim for a Methodist presbyteral line from Cedarholm cannot stand, since the ministers themselves had no intention or understanding that there was a sacramental lineage to be passed. Self-understood Protestant ordinations do not fulfill the Augustinian requirement for ordination to Orders, and one cannot, for the same reason, even claim a consecration into such a lineage. There is no there there.

9. INNER PRIESTHOOD LINEAGES AMONG INDEPENDENT BISHOPS

THE INNER PRIESTHOOD LINEAGES are a wide-ranging and unique category. Included here are both esoteric lines deriving from personal spiritual commissioning, and "hidden" apostolic lines. Many of these lineages arose during a period of about 100 years that coincide with the heyday of the initiatic Lodge systems in Western Europe and Great Britain.

I include these lines for two simple reasons:

Most bishops in the Independent Sacramental Movement have one or more of these Inner lines inextricably woven through their own lineage (and we'll look at how this can be when we consider each line).

Successors to the originating bishops count themselves as bishops in (esoteric) succession from these visionary leaders, and so we recognize the documented and identifiable succession. Further, since most of these lines have continued to hold to the teachings and practices first taught, there is demonstrable succession of Tradition as well as succession of Bishops.

It is important to note that the founding bishops of esoteric lines often received their commissioning and Orders directly in visionary and/or mystical encounters with non-corporeal sources during structured spiritual events. The hallmarks of true commissioning and consecration have been evident to those contemporaries of the founding elders / bishops. In this, these leaders are close kin to St. Paul and his Damascus Road experience: Paul became an Apostle through direct visionary commissioning. In several of these lineages, apostolic succession has been added into the esoteric lineage, "regularizing" the Orders of the esoteric church.

In other cases, bishops claim continuance from obscure or otherwise hidden apostolic source, whose historic details cannot be verified by conventional means. These newly-revealed lineages have also tended to feature a visionary and/or mystical aspect, or discovery event. Passage into the particular succession is sometimes tightly controlled. As with the other group of lineages, conventional apostolic succession has sometimes been added into the Inner Priesthood lineage, "regularizing" the Orders of the church.

We must recognize that for the lineages in this section, apostolic succession was not deemed necessary for the communities founded and organized around the inner priesthood consecrations. However, a number of such esoteric Christian communities have found that apostolic orders have enriched and expanded their faith journeys. We would be in error to suggest that the apostolic lineages lend "legitimacy" to such inner priesthood communities—and should recognize that this would be, in fact, just a version of the validity argument!

It must remain a respectful point of discussion whether a non-corporeal consecration event can be considered an apostolic ordination. This is an intriguing topic worthy of its own exploration.

Note: We confine ourselves in this chapter to the discussion of churches that self-identify as Christian. This chapter will not include the Thelemic bodies (originating from the visionary and non-Christian ceremonial magickal work of Aleister Crowley). The original Ecclesia Gnostica Catholica (EGC), and its several newer generations of Thelemic churches who have broadened their approach into more classic Gnosticisms are certainly not conventionally Christian, and by most thoughtful definitions of Gnosticism are not Christian Gnostics. And yet some of these descendents of Thelemic philosophy are also intermixing clearly Christian elements—this whole grouping of Churches deserves further discovery and discussion in its own right.

I must continue in the spirit of full disclosure that I began this book: I am in fact also a founding bishop of a line of succession originating in a consecration from an angel in 1974 during a community Eucharistic event. That particular Inner Priesthood succession was given for the founding of the Graal Church, which remained a private initiatic church until 2004. We'll look at this in more detail at the end of this chapter.

I am deeply grateful to +John Plummer and +Philip Garver for the information and insights they provided for the descriptions and lineages in this section. And I welcome any additional insights, lineage information, and discussion, and will post to my website at pelagios.net/ismpage.html.

I present these groups with a great deal of affection and admiration for their courage and creativity.

CATHOLIC APOSTOLIC CHURCH ("IRVINGITES")

Rev. Edward Irving (1792–1834) was a Scottish Presbyterian minister. He was an articulate advocate for Pre-Millenarianism, manifested in miraculous healings, the gift of tongues, and prophesying. These he understood as signs of the beginning of the "end times," and he preached Christ's imminent return. He was committed to following received prophecies, and to fostering spiritual healing and the gift of tongues among his congregation. This activity led to his eventual dismissal and excommunication from the Presbyterian Church. He took most of his enthusiastic congregation with him, and began meeting in a rented hall in London. By the end of his life, six other congregations had allied with him.

Irving's teachings and work set in motion the discernment by his followers to found the Catholic Apostolic Church in 1835, the year after his death. In fact, Irving apparently had no direct hand in the founding of this Church, but his name has been linked to it from the beginning. The naming of the Church intended to convey that it was a body for all Christians, founded in the apostolic faith. Prophecy received by the community directed the new Church to refound the office of Apostle as a condition of inviting this end time. Twelve Apostles were called forth from the communities of the new Church—these fulfilled the role of bishop for the community. The Church's liturgy morphed from Calvinist to a melding of Orthodox, Roman, and Anglican rites. The original Irvingite Church died out in the first decade of the 1900s as a result of a prophetically inspired decision to not replace the original Apostles upon their deaths. With no Apostles to make new clergy, the community could not worship once no clergy remained. This decision resulted in a schism of the German branch, calling itself The New Apostolic Church. This German group remains active to this day.

1. Edward Irving on 1 April 1868 consecrated as Angel (Bishop): 2. Francis Valentine Woodhouse, who in 1872 consecrated as Angel (Bishop): 3. Isaac Capadose, who in ? consecrated as Angel (Bishop): 4. Johann Brugger for the Restored Catholic Apostolic Church of Berne, Switzerland, who on 3 June 1924 assisted Pierre Gaston Vigue in consecrating: 5. Aloysius Stumpfl, Mar Timotheos II, for the Orthodox Missionbischof who on 28 June 1947 consecrated *sub conditione:* 6. Charles Leslie Saul, Archbishop of Suthronia in the Eparchy of all the Britons, who on 14 July 1947 consecrated *sub conditione:* 7. Hugh George de Willmott Newman, Mar Georgius I, Patriarch of Glastonbury and Catholicos of the West. On 25 October 1953 he consecrated: 8. Ronald Powell, a.k.a. Richard John Cretien, Duc de Palatine, Pre-Nicene Gnostic Catholic Church, who on September 13, 1974 consecrated *sub conditione:* 9. Mikhael Francis Augustine Itkin, who on September 21, 1980 exchanged consecrations with: 10. Joseph Vredenburgh, Mar Narsai, Patriarch of the Federation of St. Thomas Christians on July 26, 2001, assisted by Virginia Vredenburgh, Mart'a Virginia, and Joseph Eaton, Mar Tooma II consecrated: 11. Robert Angus Jones.

PRE-NICENE GNOSTIC CATHOLIC (DE PALATINE)

Richard, Duc de Palatine (a.k.a. Ronald Powell) founded the Brotherhood and Order of the Pleroma in the early 1950s, in England, to promote his vision of a restored sacramental Gnostic practice. He also founded the Pre-Nicene Gnostic Catholic Church, bringing this jurisdiction (along with the Order) to the United States in 1959. The Church body was created solely for the use of the membership of the Order.

The English Gnostic School, as it came to be known, was self-defined as Gnostic Christian. It grew out of a Liberal Catholic ethos, which was revised into a specifically Gnostic path. It uses a modified version of the Tridentine liturgy, and incorporates selections from the Nag Hammadi library as well as Manichean and other texts into its lectionary. The Church retains apostolic succession through the Ferrette and Vilatte lines, as well as the traditional 7 sacraments, which are interpreted in a Gnostic framework. Through de Palatine, the English Gnostic transmission was brought to the United States:

Apostolic Line to de Palatine. Mar Ighnatiyus Butrus IV, Metropolitan of Emesa (Homs), afterwards Syrian Orthodox Patriarch of Antioch and All the East, with approval of Moran Mar Ighnatiyus Ya'qub II, Syrian Orthodox Patriarch of Antioch and All the East, on 2 June 1866 consecrated: 1. Raimond (Jules) Ferrette, Mar Julius, Bishop of Iona for the Syrian Orthodox Patriarchate, who in 6 March 1874 consecrated: 2. Richard Williams Morgan, Mar Morien I, 1st British Patriarch, Ancient British Church, who in 1877, assisted by Frederick George Lee, Thomas Wimberly Mossman, and John Seccombe, consecrated: 3. Charles Isaac Stevens, Mar Theophilos I, 2nd British Patriarch, Ancient British Church, who on 4 May 1890, assisted by A. S. Richardson of the Reformed Episcopal Church consecrated *sub conditione*: 4. Leon Checkemian, Mar Leon, 3rd British Patriarch of the Ancient British Church and First Primus of the Free Protestant Episcopal Church (also Armenian Uniate Titular Bishop of Malatia), who on 2 November 1897 consecrated: 5. Andrew Charles Albert McLaglen, Mar Andries, 4th British

Patriarch of the Ancient British Church and Titular Bishop of Claremont, FPEC (also Primate of the United Armenian Catholic Church) who on 4 June 1922 consecrated *sub conditione:* 6. Herbert James Monzani-Heard, Mar Jacobus II, 5th British Patriarch of the Ancient British Church and Archbishop of Selsey, and Primus of the Free Protestant Episcopal Church (also Primate of the United Armenian Catholic Church). Primus Heard passed the primacy for the Ancient British Church and the United Armenian Catholic Church to Hugh George de Willmott Newman, Mar Georgius on 29 January 1945. Mar Georgius became the 6th British Patriarch. The primacy of the Free Protestant Episcopal Church was passed to William Hall. Heard, on 13 June 1943 consecrated: 7. William Bernard Crow, Mar Basilius Abdullah III, afterwards elected Patriarch of Antioch of the Ancient Orthodox Catholic Rite, Grand Master of the Order of Holy Wisdom, O.T.O./Ecclesia Gnostica Catholica, who on 10 April 1944 consecrated: 8. Hugh George de Willmott Newman, Mar Georgius I, Patriarch of Glastonbury and Catholicos of the West. On 25 October 1953 he consecrated:

Comingling with the Gnostic Priesthood. 1. Ronald Powell, a.k.a. Richard John Cretien, Duc de Palatine, Pre-Nicene Gnostic Catholic Church, who on 8 October 1958 consecrated *sub conditione*: 2. George William Boyer, Sanctuary of the Gnosis, who on 25 November 1984 consecrated: 3. Bryn Franklin (Donald Read), who, assisted by Katherine Kurtz, in December 1991 consecrated: 4. Kim-Thomas Langridge, who, assisted by Bryn Franklin, on 8 March 1992 consecrated: 5. David P. Goddard (Serapion), who, assisted by Marilyn Seig and Evelyn Hill, on 6 December 2000 consecrated: 6. Sharon Hart, who on 7 November 2001 consecrated: 7. John Paul Aloysius Plummer for the Mission Episcopate of the Theophany, who on 16 June 2002 exchanged consecrations with: 8. Robert Angus Jones.

GUILD OF THE MASTER JESUS/ CHURCH OF THE GRAAL (DION FORTUNE)

The Guild of the Master Jesus, later renamed the Church of the Graal, was founded in London by Violet Mary Firth, better known by her nom-de-plume "Dion Fortune" (1890-1946), around 1928. Fortune was yet another former Theosophist who founded her own esoteric organization called the Society of the Inner Light (SIL).

The celebrants of the Guild mass were all initiates of the Society of the Inner Light (and thus had been through a ceremonial initiation in which serious spiritual and quite priestly commitments were undertaken), but there was no separate priesthood. Fortune writes:

"...we say to you, 'Come to one of our services and see whether or not our celebration of the Eucharist gives you a sense of spiritual power you seek.' This is the only satisfactory test...when the validity of Apostolic Succession is argued in opposition to living spiritual contacts, one can best reply by calling to mind the evidence of history and pointing to the record of the Papacy during the Middle Ages. If that is the line by means of which succession to the legal rights of St. Peter must come down to us, one can only compare it to having lunatic and syphilitic ancestors in one's pedigree. Surely one is better off with honest red blood and no pretensions, than such hues in one's veins?" (From "Guild of the Master Jesus," in Charles Fielding and Carr Collins, *The Story of Dion Fortune.*)

Despite such valiantly Donatist sentiments, one should note that a Liberal Catholic priest, W. Ernest Butler (1898-1978), was involved in the Guild from its beginning. Butler was often the lector (with Charles Loveday as celebrant). One cannot help suspecting that Fr. Butler's presence reassured those concerned with sacramental technicalities. Of course, the above-referenced "lunatic and syphilitic ancestors" were promptly grafted onto this spiritual family tree. Many significant initiates of the Society of the Inner Light (and the various esoteric orders descended from it) are priests or bishops in apostolic succession, and the Guild mass is used today in both independent catholic churches, and SIL-derived esoteric groups.

Dion Fortune, who on ? "consecrated": Arthur Chichester, who on ? 1959 "consecrated": Basil Wilby (aka Gareth Knight), who on ? "consecrated": Mark Nicholas Whitehead, who on 15 August 1999 "consecrated": e. John Paul Aloysius Plummer for the

Mission Episcopate of the Theophany, who on 16 June 2002, using the form of the Guild mass exchanged consecrations with: f. Robert Angus Jones.

Note: This "consecration" is not performed as an ordination ritual, per se, but conveys a succession which usually takes place in the established ritual context of an initiation into the "Greater Mysteries."

EGLISE CATHOLIQUE GALLICANE (HOUSSAY)

At the turn of the 20th century, France's Third Republic was in dispute with the Roman Catholic Church. Archbishop Vilatte arrived at an understanding with the French politicians in an attempt to rally the Gallican school of Roman Catholic thought and institute the Catholic Apostolic Gallican Church in opposition to Rome. While this original objective was a failure, this lineage almost immediately allied itself with the vitality of the French Gnostic Revival, through the activities of Abbe Julio, Ernest Houssay, providing apostolic orders to the Gnostic churches. Abbe Julio was reknowned for his healing abilities, and much of his esoteric work on exorcisms and the use of psalms survives and is still being used by l'Eglise Gnostique Apostolique.

Line through Bricaud. 1. Antonio Francisco Xavier Alvares, Mar Julius I, Archbishop of Ceylon, Goa and India for the Malankara Jacobite Syrian Church, who at the direction of Moran Mar Ighnatiyus Butrus IV, Syrian Orthodox Patriarch of Antioch and All the East, and assisted by Paulos Mar Athanasius, on 29 May 1892 consecrated: 2. Joseph Rene Vilatte, Mar Timotheos, Archbishop of North America, who on 6 May 1900 consecrated: 3. Paolo Miraglia Gulotti, Italian National Episcopal Church, who on 4 December 1904, assisted by Joseph Rene Vilatte, consecrated: 4. Ernest Louis Rene Houssay, Mar Julius, Bishop of the Catholic Apostolic Gallican Church, who on 21 June 1911 consecrated: 5. Louis Marie Francois Giraud, Archbishop of Almyra, Gallican Patriarch, Eglise Catholique Gallicane, who on 21 July (or 25 January) 1913 consecrated: 6. Jean Bricaud, Tau Jean II, Eglise Catholique Gnostique (he had been consecrated by Encausse in 1911), who on 5 May 1918 consecrated: 7. Victor

Alfred Blanchard, Tau Targelius, who on ? 1945 consecrated: 8. Dr. Eduard Gesta, who on ? 1948 consecrated: 9. Rene Chambellant, who on ? consecrated: 10. Gilbert Tappa, Tau Gilbertus, who on 3 June 2003 consecrated: 11. Phillip Andrew Garver, Tau Vincent II, Eglise Gnostique Apostolique, who on 13 March 2004 exchanged consecrations with: 12. John Paul Aloysius Plummer, Mission Episcopate of the Theophany, who on 5 May 2006 exchanged consecrations with James Bryant, Holy Orthodox Catholic Church of America and: 13. Robert Angus Jones.

Line through Malvy. 5. Louis Marie Francois Giraud, Archbishop of Almyra, Gallican Patriarch, Eglise Catholique Gallicane, who on 2 February 1930 consecrated: 6. Bernard Isidore Jalbert-Ville, Bishop of Almyra, Eglise Catholique Gallicane, who on 12 August 1951 consecrated: 7. Jean Rene Angel Malvy, for the Eglise Catholique Apostolique et Gallicane, who on 20 February 1955 consecrated: 8. Charles Maria Joseph Poncelin d'Eschevannes (Irenaeus), Primate, Sainte Eglise Catholique Gallicane Autocephale, who on 5 May 1957 consecrated: 9. Jean-Pierre Danyel, Mar Tugual I, Primate, Sainte Eglise Celtique, who on 15 August 1966, assisted by Auguste Suliac Monier and F. Chelian, consecrated: 10. John Nicholas Collins, Liberal Catholic Church, later Old Roman Catholic Church of Canada, who on 15 December 1968, assisted by Donald Garner, English Catholic Church, consecrated: 11. Aelred Terence Peter Coghlan Distin, Holy Celtic Church, who on 26 April 1969 consecrated: 12. Anthony Walter John Williams, Primate, Holy Celtic Church, who on 20 May 1979 consecrated: 13. Thomas Illtyd Thomas, Primate, Celtic Catholic Church, who on 10 August 1986, assisting William Harry Daw and Thomas D. J. McCourt in consecrating: 14. Donald William Mullan, Christ Catholic Church International, who on 21 November 1999, assisted by L. M. McFerran and Jerome Robben consecrated: 15. Richard O. Blalack, Diocese of the Good Shepherd, Christ Catholic Church International, who on 11 July 2004 exchanged consecrations with Timothy Michael Cravens, Independent Catholic Christian Church, Peter Paul Brennan, Prime Bishop of the Ecumenical

Catholic Diocese of America, and with: 16. John Paul Aloysius Plummer, Mission Episcopate of the Theophany, who on 5 May 2006 exchanged consecrations with James Bryant of the Holy Orthodox Catholic Church of America and with: 17. Robert Angus Jones.

L'EGLISE JOHANNITE DES CHRETIENS PRIMITIFS & KNIGHTS TEMPLAR

There are several conflicting accounts of the origin of this Church, which arose out of the extraordinarily fertile explorations (and murky cross-pollenizations) of esoteric groups and independent churches in France in the 1800s. Following is a brief sketch of the generally agreed points.

The public face of the Johannite Templars began in L'Ordre du Temple in 1811 in France. This order circulated a document, the Charter of Larmenius, as part of the materials of the higher degrees in the order. This Charter contained a succession of Templarism from the founding of the order in 1118, originating from a small Gnostic faction in an Eastern or Byzantine Catholic rite, whose line came down to Raymond Fabre Palaprat, the Grand Master of the order.

The first part of the Charter is purported to have been written in Greek in 1154, and claimed that the original Templar Commanders were secret initiates of Gnostic Christians under the leadership of Patriarch Theoclete, who had made Hugh de Payans heir to the apostolic succession of John the Divine. The Charter further related a secret legend of succession from Moses through Christ. Moses was said to have gained certain Gnostic initiation from the Magi of Egypt, transmitting this down through Essene discipleship and on to Christ. It must be noted that the Charter was examined at the time by the British Museum, which concluded that the inks used to write the Charter were inconsistent with the dates given for the writing—so at least part of the Charter was deemed a forgery.

This church used a Bogomil version of John's Gospel called the Evangelikon. It is unclear, however, whether this church bears any direct antecedents in actual Mandean or Johannite Gnostic groups. The EGA purports that the Evangelikon is a mistranslation of the Greek word for a commentary on the Gospel (Evangelion), and in agreement with the noted historian Jean Markale, that the "secrets" of the Templars stemmed from the Ancient Oriental Orthodox Church they encountered in Jerusalem.

Archbishop Bertil Persson has recovered the following succession for the Johannites: 1. Pope Benedict XIII (Pietro Francesco Vincenzo Maria Orsini de Gavina) on 19 March 1726 consecrated: 2. Melchior de Polignac, Bishop of Bensacon, who on 11 September 1735 consecrated: 3. Antonius Petrus de Grammont II, Bishop of Basel for L'Eglise Catholique de la France, who on 21 November 1744 consecrated: 4. Josephus Guilemus Rink von Baldenstein, Bishop of Lausanne for the Katholische Kirke Deutschland, who on 1 April 1759 consecrated: 5. Josephus Nicolaus de Montenach, Bishop of Lydda for L'Eglise Catholique de la France, who on 22 March 1772 consecrated: 6. Jean Baptiste Gobel, Bishop of Paris for L'Eglise Constitutionelle, who on 27 March 1791 consecrated: 7. Antoine-Adrien Lamourette, Bishop of Lyons for L'Eglise Constitutionelle, who on 4 April 1791 consecrated: 8. Jean Baptiste Royer, Bishop of Belley, who on 3 August 1800 consecrated: 9. Guillaume Mauviel, Bishop of Santo Domingo, Haiti and later Primate of L'Eglise Johannites des Chretiens Primitifs (a church closely associated with the Knights Templar), who on 29 July 1810 consecrated *sub conditione*: 10. Bernard Fabre-Palaprat, Patriarch of L'Eglise Johannites des Cretiens Primitifs. He was also Grand Master of the Ordo Supremus Militaris Templi Hierosolymitani (OSMTH—Knights Templar). He on ? consecrated: 11. Bernard Clement, who on ? consecrated: 12. Jean Bricaud, Tau Jean II, Eglise Catholique Gnostique (he had been consecrated by Encausse in 1911), who on 5 May 1918 consecrated: 13. Victor Alfred Blanchard, Tau Targelius, who on ? 1945 consecrated: 14. Dr. Eduard Gesta, who on ? 1948 consecrated: 15. Rene Chambellant, who on ? consecrated: 16. Gilbert Tappa, Tau Gilbertus, who on 3 June 2003 consecrated: 17. Phillip Andrew Garver, Tau Vincent II, Eglise Gnostique Apostolique, who on 13 March 2004 exchanged consecrations with: 18. John Paul Aloysius Plummer, Mission Episcopate of the Theophany, who on 5 May 2006 exchanged consecrations with James Bryant, Holy Orthodox Catholic Church of America and: 19. Robert Angus Jones. (Note: See updated report on this lineage at www.pelagios.net/succession.pdf)

OEUVRE DE LA MISERICORDE/ EGLISE DE MONT CARMEL (VINTRAS)

Eugene Vintras founded the "Work of Mercy" (l'Oeuvre de la Misericorde) in 1839 to proclaim visionary communications from the Archangel Michael, the Holy Ghost, St. Joseph and the Virgin Mary. Vintras learned through these visions that he was the reincarnation of the prophet Elijah. After four years of evangelizing and five years of imprisonment, he founded the "Interior Sanctuary of the Elie of Carmel" or the Eliate Church of Carmel. Vintras is also recorded as having performed a number of miracles.

Erroneously labeled a Satanist by his foes, Vintras' Church is more a French parallel to the Irvingites (elsewhere in this chapter). Vintras attracted several Irvingite priests into his fold. Both Churches arose at the same time, and as part of a larger "movement" of individuals and groups towards direct mystical encounter with the Divine. Abbe Boullan—himself a notorious Satanist and expert in black arts—seized control of the Church after Vintras' death, and the majority of the faithful left for other groups. It is commonly held that the authority for the Vintrasian Church was subsumed into the Patriarchate of Jean Bricaud of the Gnostic Church, along with the Johannite Church.

1. Eugene Vintras on ? consecrated: 2. Marius Breton, who in 1908 consecrated: 3. Jean Bricaud (see Doinel lines).

EGLISE GNOSTIQUE (DOINEL)

The Eglise Gnostique was inaugurated as the result of a series of spirit communications received by Jules Doinel in 1888. He contacted discarnate Bogomil bishops, who commissioned him to restore the Gnostic Church. During these communications,

Doinel was spiritually consecrated "Bishop of Montsegur and Primate of the Albigenses" at the hands of the "Eon Jesus" and two Bogomil bishops.

Doinel, a librarian and an antiquarian of note, thoroughly researched the Cathar (and their Gnostic predecessors) roots of his refounded Church, and imbued the Eglise Gnostique with Cathar doctrine and liturgical structure.

Doinel's Church was formed in a matrix of tremendous esoteric gnostic ferment on the Continent. The story of the growth and evolution of The Eglise Gnostique, its developments and renamings and schisms and national variants and reunions, is too long to tell here. The names of the various groups are retained in the lineage below, to provide indication of particular evolution or alignment of each bishop and provide leads to further reading. An excellent history of the churches stemming from Doinel is at: *www.eglisegnostique.org/history.htm.*

Two pertinent factors concerning the Eglise Gnostique must be noted: **First**—almost from the beginning, Doinel's church and its successors were allied in various ways with the nascent Martinist (and other initiatic) movements. **Second**—at various points, Doinel's church (and its successors) was infused with apostolic succession from the Syrian Gallican Church (of the Vilatte succession via Houssay's Gallican Church).

Doinel and his successors introduced the use of the title "Tau" in distinction to the Eastern/Syrian use of "Mar" to designate their bishops. Tau signifies both the Greek Tau Cross, of ancient Christian usage, and the Egyptian Ankh cross, also used by some early Christian communities—though here more an allusion to the ancient Mysteries of Egypt. This title has become the common title for all Gnostic bishops, even those who have diverged from tradition and now consider themselves to be non-Christian.

The following lines chart some of the proliferation of the French Gnostic succession from Bishop Doinel and his original Eglise Gnostique Universelle, down to the Ecclesia Gnostica Apostolica, the US French Gnostic jurisdiction.

Line of Direct Succession within the French Tradition. 1. Jules-Benoit Stanislas Doinel du Val-Michel (Jules Doinel), Tau

Valentin II, who on 14 September 1892 consecrated: 2. Gerard Encausse (Papus), Tau Vincent, Bp. of Toulouse, Eglise Gnostique, who on ? 1910 consecrated: 3. Jean Bricaud, Tau Jean II, Patriarch, Eglise Catholique Gnostique (he had been consecrated by Fabre des Essarts in 1901 as Bp. of Lyon, by Breton of the Vintras Church in 1908, and by Encausse in 1911, and by Clement of the Johannite Templars—uniting in himself the Doinel, Vintras, and Palaprat lineages; he had also been consecrated by Louis Giraud of the Vilatte line through the Eglise Catholique Gallicane), who on 5 May 1918 consecrated: 4. Victor Alfred Blanchard, Tau Targelius, who on ? 1945 consecrated: 5. Dr. Edouard Gesta, who on ? 1948 consecrated: 6. René Chambellant, Tau Renatus, Patriarch, who on ? consecrated: 7. Gilbert Tappa, Tau Gilbertus, Primary successor to Chambellant, acting Patriarch, who on 3 June 2003 consecrated: 8. Phillip Andrew Garver, Tau Vincent II, Eglise Gnostique Apostolique, who on 13 March 2004 exchanged consecrations with: 9. John Paul Aloysius Plummer, Mission Episcopate of the Theophany, who on 5 May 2006 exchanged consecrations with James Bryant, Holy Orthodox Catholic Church of America and: 10. Robert Angus Jones.

Line through Mauchel. 1. Jules-Benoit Stanislas Doinel du Val-Michel (Jules Doinel), Tau Valentin II, who in 10 December 1892 consecrated: 2. Lucien Mauchel, Tau Bardesanes, Bp. of La Rochelle & Saintes, Eglise Gnostique, who in 1930 consecrated: 3. Henri Meslin de Champigny, Tau Harmonius, Eglise Gnostique Universelle, (he was also consecrated in 1930 by Victor Blanchard, who conveyed the Syrian Gallican lineage) who on 10 June 1946 consecrated: 4. Robert Ambelain, Tau Jean III, Eglise Gnostique Universelle, later Eglise Gnostique Apostolique (Ecclesia Gnostica Apostolica), who on 26 May 1958 consecrated: 5. Roger Pommery, Tau Jean IV, Eglise Gnostique Apostolique, who on 16 September 1967 consecrated: 6. Willer Vital-Herne, Tau Guillaume, Ecclesia Gnostica Apostolica, who on 7 September 1970 consecrated: 7. Roger St. Victor Herard, Tau Charles I, Ecclesia Gnostica Catholica Apostolica, who on 4 November 1984 consecrated: 8. Robert Michael Cokinis, Tau

Charles Harmonius II, who on 10 November 2002 consecrated: 9. Phillip Andrew Garver, Tau Vincent II, Eglise Gnostique Apostolique, who on 13 March 2004 exchanged consecrations with: 10. John Paul Aloysius Plummer, Mission Episcopate of the Theophany, who on 5 May 2006 exchanged consecrations with James Bryant, Holy Orthodox Catholic Church of America and: 11. Robert Angus Jones.

ANCIENT GNOSTIC CHURCH OF ELEUSIS (PEITHMAN)

The clearest indication of the genesis of E.C.H. Peithman's Ancient Gnostic Church of Eleusis is that in the opening decades of the 1900s, Peithman (along with the rest of the world) read with great interest the newly-published translations of the Pistis Sophia and other classical Gnostic writings. While the overall understanding of the great Gnostic schools was as yet quite meager, it proved to be revolutionary. These writings deeply inspired Peithman, and after writing his own Gnostic Catechism, he announced the formation of his new Church. While similar to the work of Doinel and the French Gnostics, Peithman's Church was a unique expression of the gnosis.

1. Ernst Christian Heinrich Peithman, Basilides, in 1930 consecrated: 2. Arnoldo Krumm-Heller, Tau Huirachoca, who on ? consecrated: 3. Johannes Muller Rider, Sar Thelemako, who in 1976 consecrated: 4. Roberto de la Caridad Toca y Medina (also consecrated by Spruit 15 Sept. 1982), who on 6 January 1985 assisted Roger St. Victor Herard, Tau Charles I, Ecclesia Gnostica Apostolica, in consecrating: 5. Jorge Enrique Rodriguez-Villa, who on 30 October 1999, assisted by Antonio Mathieu and Jurgen Bless, consecrated: 6. Valdiveso Matthews, who on 9 September 2001 consecrated: 7. Phillip Andrew Garver, Tau Vincent II, Eglise Gnostique Apostolique, who on 13 March 2004 exchanged consecrations with: 8. John Paul Aloysius Plummer, Mission Episcopate of the Theophany, who on 5 May 2006 exchanged consecrations with James Bryant, Holy Orthodox Catholic Church of America and: 9. Robert Angus Jones.

GNOSTISCHE KATHOLISCHE KIRCHE, G. K. K. (REUSS)

There is no documentary evidence to indicate the origin of Reuss' episcopacy. General consensus believes that at a general conference of illuminati and various initiatic traditions (and Gnostics) in 1908 in France, that Gerard Encaussse (Papus) of the Doinel lineage, exchanged dignities and lineages with Reuss. It is known that after this conference, Reuss was acknowledged as a national leader of Doinel's Church (at that time named Eglise Gnostique Catholique—Ecclesia Gnostica Catholica), for Germany, and his Church's name is the German translation of the original EGC name.

Under Reuss, the GKK first was considered to be the sacramental and liturgical expression of a new fraternal order he founded, the Ordo Templi Orientis (OTO). The GKK/EGC (and OTO) under Reuss has little correlation to the later Thelemic rescension of the OTO and EGC by Aleister Crowley.

Jules-Benoit Stanislas Doinel du Val-Michel (Jules Doinel), Tau Valentin II, who on 1898 consecrated: Gerard Encausse (Papus), Tau Vincent, Eglise Gnostique, who in 1908 consecrated: 1. Theodor Reuss (Peregrinus), in 1908 consecrated: 2. Arnoldo Krumm-Heller, Tau Huirachoca, who on ? consecrated: 3. Johannes Muller Rider, Sar Thelemako, who in 1976 consecrated: 4. Roberto de la Caridad Toca y Medina (also consecrated by Spruit 15 Sept. 1982), who on 6 January 1985 assisted Roger St. Victor Herard, Tau Charles I, Ecclesia Gnostica Apostolica, in consecrating: 5. Jorge Rodriguez-Villa, Tau Johannes XXIII, who in 1996 consecrated: 6. Edmundo Pellizari, Tau Vladimir, who on 9 May 1998 consecrated *sub conditione*: 7. John Paul Aloysius Plummer for the Mission Episcopate of the Theophany, who on 16 June 2002 exchanged consecrations with: 8. Robert Angus Jones.

Alleged Line from Aleister Crowley. There is ongoing debate concerning whether Aleister Crowley had received an Apostolic or Gnostic consecration from Reuss, and thus whether he did or was able to convey an Apostolic or Gnostic consecration to Crow. There are documents from Crowley to Crow that indicate *something* was conveyed. I present this possible line here for the sake of completeness in the absence of clear evidence one way or the other.

Theodor Reuss (Peregrinus), who in 1912 is said to have consecrated: Edward Alexander (Aleister) Crowley, who in August 1944 declared (and is claimed to have consecrated): 3. William Bernard Crow, as "Sovereign Patriarch of the Gnostic Catholic Church & Vicar of Solomon," who on 3 September 1944 consecrated: 4. Henry George Brook, who on 20 May 1945 exchanged consecrations with H.C. Bartlett, F.E. Langhelt, John Syer, and Hugh George de Wilmott Newman (Mar Georgius I, Patriarch of Glastonbury and Catholicos of the West). 5. Hugh George de Willmott Newman, who on 25 October 1953 consecrated: 6. Ronald Powell, Richard Duc de Palatine of the Pre-Nicene Church, who on 7 April 1967 consecrated: 7. Baron Stephan A. von Hoeller-Bertam, *Tau Stephanus I*, Ecclesia Gnostica, who on 10 November 2002 consecrated: 8. Phillip Andrew Garver, *Tau Vincent II*, Eglise Gnostique Apostolique, who on 13 March 2004 exchanged consecrations with: 9. John Paul Aloysius Plummer, Mission Episcopate of the Theophany, who on 5 May 2006 exchanged consecrations with James Bryant, Holy Orthodox Catholic Church of America and: 10. Robert Angus Jones.

EGLISE GNOSTIQUE UNIVERSELLE (BRICAUD / CHEVILLON)

(Edited from a narrative by Philip Garver) +Chevillon succeeded +Bricaud as Patriarch of +Bricaud's Eglise Catholique Gnostique, which had become the Eglise Gnostique Universelle, until his assassination by Nazi collaborator authorities on 22 March 1944. There is no record of any consecrations performed by +Chevillon prior to his death, other than the ordination of four deacons. One of the four deacons, René Chambellant, was elected to succeed Chevillon as Patriarch. Chambellant, as the duly elected successor to Chevillon needed to be consecrated, and although an agreement had been made between Chevillon and a certain bishop Marie-Marcel Laemmer and two other bishops between 1940 and 1941, Laemmer was the only one not opposed to the consecration of a Gnostic. To resolve this dilemma, a bishop named Dr. Edouard Gesta, who had himself been consecrated by Victor Blanchard in 1945, agreed to make this possible. This was well received, since Chevillon was the successor to Bricaud, and Blanchard had been consecrated by Bricaud, so the succession of the Gnostic, Johannite, Vintrasian Carmelite, and Apostolic streams were all continued.

While +Chambellant had the support of most, there was contention amongst the other three deacons of Chevillon (see section on Eglise Gnostique Apostolique). +Chambellant was called away to Africa on business, and upon his return, discovered that there had been much activity in the church founded by Ambelain, and not desiring to cause further political distress, did not assert himself as the legitimate Patriarch (although this was known by many), and adopted the name of the Eglise Gnostique Apostolique for the use of his own line. Upon his return, +Chambellant entered into an agreement with a Mariavite Bishop named +Jean-Paul Bonnerot, and subsequently named him as successor to the legitimate patriarchate of the Gnostic Church. However, after some years, +Bonnerot dropped out of sight, and +Chambellant, learning of his lapse in Masonic qualifications, wrote a Patriarchal notice deposing him as successor with any rights to the Church. +Bonnerot did not even make an appearance at the time of the passing of +Chambellant. To rectify the lack of succession to the legitimate patriarchate, +Chambellant performed three consecrations: Jean Gautier, Christian Fella. and Gilbert Tappa. These three served as a "college," but Tappa was seen as the primary bishop and was intended to succeed Chambellant as Patriarch.

On 3 June 2003, Phillip Andrew Garver signed an official accord with Gilbert Tappa, with the approbation of the "college", thus re-uniting the Gnostic church in America with the original succession of Patriarchs of Bricaud and Chevillon's Eglise Gnostique Universelle, now under the name of the Eglise Gnostique Apostolique. The ecclesiastical name of *T. Mar Sarpanim* has been reserved for Bishop +Garver, *T. Vincent II*, now assuming the status of Archbishop, for his eventual succession as the sole individual with this direct lineage.

1. Jean Bricaud, Tau Jean II, Eglise Catholique Gnostique (he had been consecrated by Fabre des Essarts in 1901 as Bp. of Lyon, by Breton of the Vintras Church in 1908, and by Encausse in 1911, and by Clement of the Johannite Templars—uniting in himself the Doinel, Vintras, and Palaprat lineages), who on 5 May 1918 consecrated: 2. Victor Alfred Blanchard, Tau Targelius, who on ? 1945 consecrated: 3. Dr. Edouard Gesta, who on ? 1948 consecrated: 4. René Chambellant, elected and enthroned Patriarch and successor to Chevillon, who on ? consecrated: 5. Gilbert Tappa, Eglise Gnostique Apostolique de France, who on 3 June 2003 consecrated: 6. Phillip Andrew Garver, Tau Vincent II, Eglise Gnostique Apostolique, who on 13 March 2004 exchanged consecrations with: 7. John Paul Aloysius Plummer, Mission Episcopate of the Theophany, who on 5 May 2006 exchanged consecrations with James Bryant, Holy Orthodox Catholic Church of America, and: 8. Robert Angus Jones.

Alleged Line from Krumm-Heller. Followers of Krumm-Heller generally claim a consecration for him at the hands of Chevillon, but this has always been disputed by the remaining members of Chevillon's church. The record is presented here in the interest of completeness.

Antonio Francisco Xavier Alvares, Mar Julius I, Archbishop of Ceylon, Goa and India for the Malankara Jacobite Syrian Church, who at the direction of Moran Mar Ighnatiyus Butrus IV, Syrian Orthodox Patriarch of Antioch and All the East, and assisted by Paulos Mar Athanasius, on 29 May 1892 consecrated: Joseph Rene Vilatte, Mar Timotheos, Archbishop of North America, who on 6 May 1900 consecrated: Paolo Miraglia Gulotti, Italian National Episcopal Church, who on 4 December 1904, assisted by Joseph Rene Vilatte, consecrated: Ernest Louis Rene Houssay, Mar Julius, Bishop of the Catholic Apostolic Gallican Church, who on 21 June 1911 consecrated: Louis Marie Francois Giraud, Archbishop of Almyra, Gallican Patriarch, Eglise Catholique Gallicane, who on 5 January 1936 consecrated: 1. Constant Chevillon, Tau Harmonius, Eglise Catholique Gnostique, who in 1939 consecrated: 2. Arnoldo Krumm-Heller, Tau Huirachoca, who on ? consecrated: 3. Johannes Muller Rider, Sar Thelemako, who in 1976 consecrated: 4. Roberto de la Caridad Toca y Medina (also consecrated by Spruit 15 Sept. 1982), who on 6 January 1985 assisted Roger St. Victor Herard, Tau Charles I, Ecclesia Gnostica Apostolica, in consecrating: 5. Jorge Rodriguez-Villa, Tau Johannes XXIII, who in 1996 consecrated: 6. Edmundo Pellizari, Tau Vladimir, who on 9 May 1998 consecrated *sub conditione*: 7. John Paul Aloysius Plummer for the Mission Episcopate of the Theophany, who on 16 June 2002 exchanged consecrations with: 8. Robert Angus Jones.

ECCLESIA GNOSTICA MYSTERIORUM (ROSAMONDE MILLER)

The Mary Magdalene Order maintains a secret existence, and traces its succession directly from Mary Magdalene, whom Tradition records traveled with Joseph of Arimathea into the West after the Resurrection, and after a time in Britain, went on to France to preach the Gospel. The Order is shepherded by a line of female bishops.

Emissaries of the bishop of the Holy Order of Miriam of Magdala (the Mary Magdalene Order) at Paris, France elected Rosamonde to the episcopate of the Order; they consecrated her in the South of France, and also conferred upon her the position of 6th and last Marashin of the Order. The Mary Magdalene lineage in the US is expressed only through the Ecclesia Gnostica Mysteriorum, at its one location in Mountain View, CA (formerly located in Palo Alto, CA).

In the MM tradition, there can be only three hierarchs at any time. I cherish this special lineage and its unique efficacy, but as with the many other lineages received, I do not claim to have any episcopal privilege in this Tradition.

Line One. Mara Celie *and* Mara Guillermine *and* Mara Simone, on 14 January 1962 consecrated: 1. Rosamonde I. Miller, Tau Rosamonde, Ecclesia Gnostica Mysteriorum, who on 24 March 1990 consecrated: 2. Katherine Kurtz, who, assisting Bryn Franklin, in December 1991 consecrated: 3. Kim-Thomas Langridge, who, assisted by Bryn Franklin, on 8 March 1992 consecrated: 4. David P. Goddard (Serapion), who, assisted by

Marilyn Seig and Evelyn Hill, on 6 December 2000 consecrated: 5. Sharon Hart, who on 7 November 2001 consecrated: 6. John Paul Aloysius Plummer for the Mission Episcopate of the Theophany, who on 16 June 2002 exchanged consecrations with: 7. Robert Angus Jones.

Line Two. 1. Rosamonde I. Miller, Tau Rosamonde, Ecclesia Gnostica Mysteriorum, who on 31 December 1982 consecrated: 2. Manuel Cabrera Lamparter, who on ? consecrated: 3. Luis Asensio Cristobal, who on 5 September 2000, assisted by Edmundo Pellizari, consecrated: 4. Emanuele Coltro-Guidi, who on 16 February 2001 consecrated: 5. Phillip Andrew Garver, Tau Vincent II, Eglise Gnostique Apostolique, who on 13 March 2004 exchanged consecrations with: 6. John Paul Aloysius Plummer, Mission Episcopate of the Theophany, who on 5 May 2006 exchanged consecrations with James Bryant, Holy Orthodox Catholic Church of America and: 7. Robert Angus Jones.

Note: Tau Rosamonde also received, and united in her episcopate, the fullness of the apostolic lines through her subconditional consecration on 18 January 1981 by +Stephan Hoeller, +Forest Barber, and +Neil Jack. Of note as well were the passing of inner priesthood lineages: the English Gnostic line from Heoller, and the French Gnostic, Cathar, and Johannite lines from Barber.

THE SACRED KING & PRIESTESS QUEEN INNER PRIESTHOOD (W.G. GRAY)

(Edited from a narrative by John Plummer.) William Gordon Gray was born on March 25, 1913 in Middlesex, England. Gray's mother (also an occultist) was Roman Catholic, and took him to mass, although he had been originally baptized in the Church of England. At his own insistence, he was baptized in the Roman Church, and even considered the priesthood.

Gray was trained and initiated by Emile Napoleon Hauenstein, who in turn was allegedly a former student of Papus. The Kabbalistic Order of the Rose Cross and Martinism are often mentioned in regard to ENH. Gray was also, much later, initiated into Dion Fortune's Society of the Inner Light, from which he quickly departed, largely due to some unfortunate notions about nation

& race in magic. (The SIL initiator was probably Arthur Chichester.) Further, Gray was associated for some time with Ronald Heaver (aka Zadok) and his Sanctuary of Avalon. It is worth noting that Gray (as initiator) did some work with another former SIL initiate, Basil Wilby (aka Gareth Knight), although they later parted company. In the eventual development of their respective work, Gray did not see the SIL initiation as most important, while Wilby did.

In the late 60s and early 70s, Gray worked with a young musician named Robert John Stewart, whom he eventually initiated into the inner priesthood he had received from Hauenstein, with the assistance of Norman Gibbs. The story of the initiation, along with much other information on Gray's life and background, can be found in *The Old Sod: The Odd Life and Inner Work of William G. Gray* by Alan Richardson and Marcus Claridge (Ignotus, 2003). Towards the end of his life, Gray founded a loosely-organized magical fraternity known as the Sangreal Sodality. Two of his initiates, Marcia Pickands and Jacobus Swart, continue to play a large role in the Sodality.

In November 1997, in New York City, John Paul Aloysius Plummer received the inner priesthood from R.J. Stewart by laying on of hands, assisted by his then-wife, Josephine Dunne. According to a private paper given at the time, the lineage "partakes of the esoteric Christian stream of spirit, but also predates it by millennia (sic)." Stewart then notes the interweaving of a threefold lineage, quoting directly from the paper:

(a) Physical initiatory line in the Western Tradition, leading back to W.G. Gray, to "Papus" in France, and to Russia in the 19th century, before which time we do not have any historical account.

(b) Non-physical initiatory line from Sacred Kingship, which links to Faery and Underworld traditions.

(c) Non-physical initiatory line of Priesthood from direct inner contacts, sometimes known as the Order of Melchizedek in esoteric traditions, though it is merely the Judeo-Christian term for something that exists everywhere, with many cultural manifestations. Both (b) and (c) are physically merged through (a).

In instruction given at the time, Josephine also noted her family background, which is partially Rom (so-called Gypsy) with a devotion to the Black Madonna, and the connection via her father to Catholic mysticism, as relevant to the transmission. Stewart also noted the connection to the Golden Dawn via Dion Fortune, and an original Golden Dawn sword was on the altar for the ceremony. In recent publications, Stewart cites Gray, Fortune, and Heaver as primary spiritual ancestors.

1. Jules-Benoit Stanislas Doinel du Val-Michel (Jules Doinel), Tau Valentin II, who on 14 September 1892 consecrated: 2. Gerard Encausse (Papus), Tau Vincent, Bp. of Toulouse, Eglise Gnostique, who on ? consecrated: 3. Emile Napoleon Hauenstein, who on ? consecrated: 4. W. G. (William Gordon) Gray, who in 1970 consecrated: 5. R. J. Stewart, who on November 1997 consecrated: 6. John Paul Aloysius Plummer for the Mission Episcopate of the Theophany, who on 16 June 2002 exchanged consecrations with: 7. Robert Angus Jones.

CHURCH OF JESUS CHRIST OF LATTER-DAY SAINTS (SMITH)

In May—June 1829, the Prophet Joseph Smith, along with Oliver Cowdery, were ordained into the restored Aaronic and Melchizedeck priesthoods, on the banks of the Susquehanna river. This occurred during a period in which Smith and his trusted senior followers were in the midst of translating the newly-received Book of Mormon. Through this dual ordination, the two directly received a restored Old Covenant (culminating in the John the Baptist) and New Covenant (passing from Melchizedek down to Christ) priesthood.

Details concerning the date(s) and circumstances of the ordinations are hotly disputed, even among Mormons. Smith and Cowdery themselves wrote conflicting reports of the events, and changed their stories over time (though some speculate they were under vows to keep the whole of the story secret at the time). Further, it was not until after 1835 that missionaries of the LDS Church claimed specific restoration from Peter, James, and John. However, the core fact of a transmission and restoration of an authoritative priesthood for the Latter Day Saints is not in doubt.

Accounts vary as to whether the Aaronic priesthood was conveyed "by an angel" or by "John the Baptist." Likewise, accounts vary as to whether the Melchizedek priesthood was conveyed "by an angel" or by the apostles "Peter, James, and John." Whatever the facts, both priesthoods were safeguarded by direct tactile succession within the Church.

William C. Conway was a Mormon High Priest of the Order of Melchizedek. At a time when Mormons were generally separating themselves from their more scandalous original beliefs (such as polygamy), Conway espoused these "fundamentalist" doctrines, but combined them with a deeply held belief in Druidism and reincarnation. In this pursuit of the merging of his Mormon beliefs and his esoteric beliefs, he met Roland Shreves.

1. William C. Conway, Mormon High Priest of the Order of Melchizedek, on 25 December 1954 consecrated: 2. Roland Merritt Shreves, who on 8 October 1967 exchanged consecrations with: 3. Michel Paul Bertiaux for the Neo-Pythagorean Gnostic Church, who on 16 June 1979 consecrated *sub conditione*: 4. Forest Ernest Barber, who on 15 June 1988 consecrated *sub conditione*: 5. Paul G. W. Schultz, who on 1 August 1992 consecrated *sub conditione*: 6. Jorge Enrique Rodriguez-Villa, who on 8 September 1997 consecrated: 7. Lawrence Stephen Terry, who on 25 April 1998 consecrated: 8. John Paul Aloysius Plummer for the Mission Episcopate of the Theophany, who on 16 June 2002 exchanged consecrations with: 9. Robert Angus Jones.

HOLY ORDER OF MANS (BLIGHTON)

(Edited from a narrative by John Plummer.) The Science of Man Church was founded on March 2, 1961 by Earl W. (Father Paul) Blighton (1904-1974), a retired electrical engineer who had migrated from upstate New York to the Bay Area of California. Blighton had studied with various theosophical, Rosicrucian, and new thought organizations, and was once (in 1963-64) an initiate of the Christian Yoga Church of Father Subramuniya (Robert Hansen). The SOM (as it is known) later gave birth to a vowed order named the Holy Order of M.A.N.S. (the HOOM, pronounced "Home"), founded on July 24, 1968, which had several thousand members in the United States before fragmenting in the early 1980s when the leadership of the Order attempted to lead it into the Orthodox Church.

Many members of the HOOM joined the Orthodox Church in 1988, becoming Christ the Saviour Brotherhood. However, the SOM continues to exist, as do several other churches and orders which use the sacramental forms of the HOOM, including the threefold initiations of baptism, illumination, and realization. Father Paul claimed to have brought forth a renewed priesthood, in which men and women were ordained equally, through inner revelation. He stated that his primary inner teacher for many years was the biblical Ananias, although he also was allegedly in communication with Jesus, Mary, and others. Many of his students claimed that Blighton was the reincarnation of the Apostle Paul, and Blighton sometimes spoke with the voice of Paul when in high mystical states. While he did not actively discourage the belief that he was Paul reincarnated, it is not clear whether he ever actually asserted this. Father Paul wrote about the objections to this priesthood, as it had no traditional authority or apostolic succession, in *The Philosophy of sacramental Initiation*:

> *"Our answer is simple and clear: We receive our authority through Jesus Christ Himself by revelation. This is a truth that we simply declare. We do not argue or discuss it, it simply is the truth. We prove it by our actions and the fruits of our labors. The proof is in the pudding; the proof is there for anyone to see in the faces and bodies of our brothers and sisters, in the regeneration and illumination that is manifest in them."*

Despite this teaching, within a generation, most of the organizations which continue the spiritual transmission of Father Paul have acquired apostolic succession. It is worth noting that the acceptance of apostolic succession did not mean the devaluation of the "Pauline" lineage from Blighton. Many of the post-HOOM groups ordain their clergy twice, using both HOOM and Catholic forms. The apostolic lineage is known to have come through the support of Harold Freeman, who conveyed the Vredenburgh lines. The Gnostic Order of Christ is one of the Orders that continue to carry this dual lineage.

The HOOM equivalent to a Catholic bishop is found in the office of Master Teacher. Only those Master Teachers who are given "the Rights of Ordination" are allowed to ordain other priests and teachers, and to pass on Father Paul's lineage. After the dissolution of the HOOM, some MTs who did not have the Rights have chosen to ordain anyway. One MT, Anthony Ruiz (Master Raeson) claimed that he received the Rights spiritually at the time of Father Paul's unexpected death. This has led to confusion, and to competing claims of validity.

Father Paul gave the Rights of Ordination to D. Wayne Harris (Master Timothy), who left the HOOM circa 1972. Some years later, Timothy began working with others, including Catherine Ann Lucas (first married name: Furbeng; second married name: Burkhouse; aka Master Jessica, later spelled Jessika). Master Jessica had been a student of one of the MTs from the original HOOM, Marian Linda Carter (Master M). Master M had ordained Jessica as a Master Teacher, although M did not hold the Rights of Ordination. Timothy later re-did Jessica's MT ordination, and (with the concurrence of Master J, Raymond Anderson, who had received the Rights from Father Paul, and is now a minister in the Church of Religious Science, Santa Rosa, CA) passed to her the Rights of Ordination. From Master M, Jessica also received the mantle of the HOOM's feminine sub-order, the Immaculate Heart Sisters of Mary, of which M had been Sister Superior. Jessica opened this transmission to both genders as the Immaculate Heart Servants of Mary.

The Gnostic Order of Christ, one of several descendent groups from the Holy Order of M.A.N.S., was founded after Fr. Paul's death in the 1970s when HOOM members went in various directions. In 1988, Bishops Timothy Harris and Jessica Lucas established the Gnostic Order of Christ to continue the HOOM teachings, while also blending in Hermetic principles with apostolic Christianity into an initiatic system.

Various bishops of HOOM also received apostolic lineage along with their esoteric initiation. It is reported that this lineage entered HOOM through the support of Harold Freeman, who conveyed the Vredenburgh lines. The Gnostic Order of Christ carries this dual lineage.

1. Nathan Colvin, who on 19 August 1985 consecrated: 2. Jessica Catherine Ann Lucas-Burkhouse and Timothy D. W. Harris, who on 19 August 2000 consecrated: 3. John Paul Aloysius Plummer for the Friends Catholic Communion, who on 16 June 2002 exchanged consecrations with: 4. Robert Angus Jones. (Note: see updated HOOM lineage at www.pelagios.net/succession.pdf)

THE GRAAL CHURCH [ECCLESIA GRADÁLIS] (JONES)

In the 1800s, at the same time that the great Hermetic Lodges, theosophical and Gnostic Churches, and the Druid and Pagan revivals were exploding onto the spiritual stage in Western Europe, a small private esoteric Christian Order was founded in Great Britain. The precise details of its founding and sources of its received teachings are not known, but they are consistent with the Western Wisdom stream, especially in its Inner Christian expressions. Some evidence suggests the Order called itself the "Ord Dyserth," old Welsh for Order of the Desert.

In 1971 the Guides of this Order determined to extend their teachings to North America. In New England they gathered together the core members and established the Somers Group. The Group members received the teachings of the first Four Gates together with Minor Orders, and began to articulate their work together as a hidden spiritual vocation. Part of the vocation of the original British Order was to work as a Hunting Lodge, investigating and resolving paranormal occurrences as a very specific sort of spiritual warfare. The Somers Group embraced this part of the vocation as well. They worked with the utmost discretion and confidentiality, and almost from the beginning were under vows to keep the existence of the Group and its teachings secret.

The Graal Church was established in 1974 at the direction of the Group's Guides. The purpose was two-fold: to provide a more focused esoteric context for members of the Somers Group to celebrate the Mysteries (sacraments); and to provide a safe structure in which to practice the more advanced teachings. On 2 February 1974 in the Group's Chapel of the Four Evangels, in Somers, Connecticut, Rob Angus Jones was called out and consecrated and anointed by an Angel to become the first American bishop of this Church.

Over the next five years, the work of the Somers Group shifted naturally into the Graal Church, and in late 1979 the Somers Group as a separate organization was formally closed in favor of the Church. But the vows of secrecy remained, so that as members left there was no means to attract new members. By the early 1980s only Jones was left, continuing the work and the teachings from the one remaining Graal Chapel. Yet work with the Church's Guides continued, producing further development and refinement of the received teachings.

In an important set of milestones for Church, in 1998 Jones was ordained an Anglican deacon and priest, and in 2001 was consecrated a bishop in the Anglican tradition. Bishop Jones also received the other major Apostolic, and Inner Priesthood and Gnostic Christian lineages, commingling the Inner and Outer Christic Mysteries, and infusing this combined inheritance into the Graal Church.

Discernment with the Church's Guides culminated in 2004 with Bishop Jones being released from the vows of secrecy taken thirty years before, with the commission to begin to make public the teachings and work. The work as Hunting Lodge was formally ended as a collective vocation of the Church, though is fully supported for those called to it. The distinctive esoteric Christian Wisdom teachings, and work on the Inner with the Church's Guides, remain central. The Graal Church protects and transmits the teachings and the unique lineage of spiritual consecration received by the Somers Group. (Current information about the Graal Church may be found on gradalis.net.)

On 2 February 1974, at the Chapel of the Four Evangels in Somers, Connecticut, an Angel initiated this line of Inner Priesthood by consecrating: Robert Angus Jones for the Graal Church (Ecclesia Gradális).

SELECT BIBLIOGRAPHY

Abba Seraphim, *Flesh of our Brethren,* British Orthodox Press, 2006.

The Anglican Independent Communion, *www.cinemaparallel.com/anglican.html*

Anson, Peter, *Bishops at Large*, Apocryphile Press, 2006.

Brandreth, Henry R. T., *Episcopi Vagantes and the Anglican Church*, Apocryphile Press, 2006.

Brennan, +Peter Paul, personal correspondence.

The British Orthodox Church, *www.uk-christian.net/boc/*

Burgess, Michael, *Lords Temporal and Lords Spiritual*, The Borgo Press, 1995.

Database of Autocephalous Bishops, Old Roman Catholic Church in North America (Wexford), *www.angelfire.com/on3/Database/*

Garver, +Philip, Eglise du Plerome web site, *www.gnostique.net* and personal correspondence.

The HarperCollins Encyclopedia of Catholicism, HarperCollins Publishers, Inc., 1995.

Hart, +Sharon, personal correspondence and conversation.

The Independent Evangelical Catholic Church in America, *www.evangelicalcatholicchurch.org* (succession detail pages no longer online).

Keizer, +Lewis, *The Wandering Bishops: Apostles of a New Spirituality*, http://hometemple.org/WanBishWeb%20Complete .pdf, 2000.

Koenig, Peter R., The Ordo Templi Orientis Phenomena Web Site, *www.cyberlink.ch/~koenig/*

The Old Catholic Church of America, *www.oldcatholic.org/*

Persson, +Bertil, personal correspondence, 2001—2004

The Apostolic Successions of the Apostolic Episcopal Church, An Outline at the Prospect of the 21st Century, 2nd revised edition, St. Ephrem's Institute, 2004.

The Apostolic Succession of the English Nonjurors and the Scottish Episcopal Church and their Role in the Formation of the Apostolic Succession of the Protestant Episcopal Church, St. Ephrem's Institute 2001.

Plummer, +John, personal correspondence.

Pruter, +Karl, J. Gordon Melton, *The Old Catholic Sourcebook*, Garland Reference Lib. of Social Science, v. 179, 1983.

Ward, Gary L, +Bertil Persson, and +Alan Bain, *Independent Bishops: An International Directory*, Detroit, MI: Apogee Books, 1990 [a.k.a., "the big red book"].

"Was Wesley Ordained a Bishop by Erasmus?," Art. V, *The Methodist Quarterly Review* 1878, *http://wesley.nnu.edu/wesleyan theology/mreview/1870/A%201878%20Was%20Wesley%20Ordained %20Bishop%20by%20Erasmus%2088-111.htm*

LINEAGE DOCUMENTS

+Peter Paul Brennan, N.D., private circulation.

+Carlos Florido (containing +Alan Stanford's succession document), N.D., private circulation.

+Denis Michel Garrison *http://www.denisgarrison.info/*

+Philip Garver, Liber Successio Apostolica, 2004, private circulation.

+James A. Johnson, 2002, private circulation.

+Rob Angus Jones, 2009, *pelagios.net/succession.pdf*

+John Kersey, N.D., private circulation.

+Kit Thomas Langridge, N.D., private circulation.

+Donald Read, N.D., private circulation.

Apostolic Succession of the Evangelical Anglican Church in America, Pub #12494-03, N.D.

Apostolica Successio Within the Evangelical Catholic Church, *http://members.aol.com/BpBarwin/index.html*

Boyle, Terrence, *http://www.tboyle.net/Catholicism/Outline.html*

Episcopal Diocese of San Joaquin: The Succession of Bishops of the Episcopal Church USA, *http://www.sjoaquin.net/sjao/listbishops.html* [note: this site is no longer online].

Duckett, Matthew, *www.ucl.ac.uk/~ucgbmxd/success.htm*

NOTES

1. This term, popularized by John Plummer in his book *The Many Paths of the Independent Sacramental Movement*, has also been used in variant forms by Richard Smoley in his book *Inner Christianity*, and by the Christengemeinschaft community. In the 1970s there was also a pioneering Synod of Independent sacramental Churches. This term (ISM) refers to a highly complex and largely undocumented phenomenon that exists in the shadows of the mainline churches. Small Orthodox, Catholic, Anglican, Lutheran, and Methodist bodies, as well as more unique communities—all of whom have received and preserve the historic episcopacy—live among us in the US and many other countries. These churches also characterize themselves as "autocephalous Orthodox" "Old Catholic" "Independent Catholic" "non-Canterbury Anglican" "Independent Anglican" and so on. They all claim to derive their episcopacy from one or more of the patriarchates of Christendom (Rome, Antioch, Alexandria, Constantinople, and Moscow).

2. As an aside, for those of you Tradition buffs: when Marriage was defined as a sacrament of the Church in around 1100 A.D., it too was defined as a one-time sacrament of initiation, giving its

own indelible character to the souls of the marriage partners. It's for this reason that so much unseemly bureaucracy has intruded on the matter of divorce and remarriage: it was crucial to preserve this sense of the indelible mark, and find ways to honor the sacrament while at the same time addressing the pastoral needs for divorce and remarriage.

In the Western Church marriage is and has always been conducted between the couple committing to marriage as the actual ministers of the sacrament; the clergy are simply witness to ensure it's properly Christian (in the Eastern Churches, the priest or bishop is required to bless the marriage covenant as minister). In fact, marriage was conducted outside on the front steps of the local church by the couple without a priest for many centuries before the Church recognized it as a sacrament.

It was about the time that the church was requiring the clergy to be celibate that the church also defined marriage as a Christian sacrament.

www.ingramcontent.com/pod-product-compliance
Lightning Source LLC
Chambersburg PA
CBHW032100080426
42733CB00006B/348

9781933993836